HAUNTED
LONDON

HAUNTED
LONDON

JAMES CLARK

TEMPUS

Frontispiece: *'Unearthly Hour'. (Andrew Rigby www.sxc.hu/profile/ the1select)*

First published 2007

Tempus Publishing
Cirencester Road, Chalford,
Stroud, Gloucestershire, GL6 8PE
www.tempus-publishing.com

Tempus Publishing is an imprint of NPI Media Group

British Library Cataloguing in Publication Data.
A catalogue record for this book is available from the British Library.

ISBN 978 0 7524 4459 8

Typesetting and origination by NPI Media Group
Printed in Great Britain

CONTENTS

ACKNOWLEDGEMENTS

My very grateful thanks to everyone who helped me put this book together and my sincere apologies to anyone I may have overlooked here: Scott Burke of The Connaughts Postcard Museum; Nick Butler, park manager of Kensington Gardens and Brompton Cemetery; John Clark, senior curator (Medieval) and deputy head of department at the Museum of London; Vanessa Crowe at the Bank of England; Richard Freeman; Dhani Hirani, reception, The Royal Parks; Chloe Holloway, office administrator, St James's Park and The Green Park; Jennie Lynch, assistant archivist, The Parliamentary Archives (House of Lords Record Office); Darren Mann from The Paranormal Database website; Alan Murdie; John Smith; Mark Wasilewski, park manager, St James's Park and The Green Park; The British Library; Merton Library Service; Tower Hamlets Local History Library and Archives; Wandsworth Libraries.

In addition, special thanks must go to the following: Jayne Ayris for looking over the typescript and offering valuable feedback, Anthony Wallis of www.ant-wallis-illustration.co.uk for creating some wonderful illustrations to use in this book, my brother Steve for making my computer behave itself, and my parents for helping in far too many ways to list.

INTRODUCTION

London must be one of the most haunted places on earth. Whichever corner you turn, whichever road or alleyway you wander down, there is a good chance you will find yourself somewhere that has been the setting for a strange tale at least once during this city's long history. And so when I was asked to write a book about London's ghost stories my first thought was, where to begin?

Depending on the definition used, 'London' can cover a vast area, and all of the various districts that comprise what is known as Greater London have their own tales to tell and merit books of their own. After much deliberation, it was decided that this book should focus specifically on the area around the centre of London, roughly from Kensington in the west to Whitechapel in the east, as this is the area that most people would recognise as being London and which tends to appear in guidebooks. (The map on page 125 shows exactly where all the stories told here are set.) But even within these boundaries it would be impossible in a book of this size to do justice to any of these fascinating stories if I tried to include all, or even most, of the literally hundreds of eerie tales in which London is steeped. Doing so would have resulted in little more than a gazetteer of the city, with insufficient room to tell the tales as they deserve to be told, and so I have not attempted this. Instead, this book concentrates mainly on ghostly tales attached to London's best-known and most important landmarks.

In the following pages you will find stories about such famous buildings as Buckingham Palace, Westminster Abbey, No. 10 Downing Street, St Paul's Cathedral and of course the Tower of London, which must surely have one of the densest populations of ghosts anywhere! In addition, there are tales about one or two places that may not be so instantly recognisable but which could not possibly be left out. Thus you will also read about one of history's most notorious haunted houses (No. 50 Berkeley Square in Mayfair) and what is probably the world's most famous haunted pub (the Grenadier in Belgravia). Finally, the concluding chapter describes the many ghost stories that came about as a result of the awful crimes of Jack the Ripper in London's 'Autumn of Terror' in 1888.

You do not have to believe in the supernatural to enjoy a good ghost story and it must be left up to the reader to decide whether to consider some or all of the tales recounted here as literally true, or to think of them more as colourful legends. Either way, they undeniably provide an enthralling perspective from which to examine this great city. And once you start looking into the stories *behind* the reports of spectres and phantoms, what an incredible history is revealed!

'The real magic of discovery,' according to Marcel Proust, 'lies not in seeking new landscapes but in having new eyes' and so, with that thought in mind, welcome to a London that will appear at the same time both familiar and strange – welcome to *Haunted London*.

James Clark,
August 2007
writer@clarkweb.co.uk

CHAPTER ONE

THE WEST: FROM KENSINGTON TO MAYFAIR

Kensington Palace

Kensington Palace has been home to many royals and it has seen many die, too. It was the death of King George II here in 1760 that led to the palace's most enduring ghostly tale.

George Augustus was born in 1683 in Hanover, a former state of north-western Germany, where he spent his early life. He was the only son of the German prince George Louis, elector of Hanover, and when his father was crowned King George I of Great Britain in 1714, the younger George was designated Prince of Wales. In 1727, he succeeded his father as King George II and he would reign for thirty-three years although for much of that time he wished he could return to his native land.

His final years were passed at Kensington Palace where, it is said, the ageing king would spend long hours gazing out of the window towards the weather vane. He was desperate to receive news from his beloved Hanover and every day would hope against hope that the wind was blowing in the right direction to speed along the ships bringing long-awaited despatches from his homeland. But the winds stayed against him, the ships were kept away from England's shores and the king's heavily accented voice could often be heard muttering in frustration, 'Vhy dond't dey kom?' At long last, the winds did change and the ships finally arrived bearing their precious despatches, but it was too late. George died an unexpected and rather undignified death at about 7.30 a.m. on 25 October 1760. Having gone to make his toilet he collapsed and cut his head against the edge of a bureau as he fell. His valet discovered him lying on the floor, a doctor was called and the king was pronounced dead, a subsequent autopsy revealing the cause of death to be a dissecting aneurism of the aorta.

According to legend, his ghost still haunts the palace, waiting for the news he never lived to hear. Sometimes, when the wind blows strongly from the west, his sad, pale face is glimpsed at a window gazing out towards the weather vane, and a mournful voice drifts through the corridors, asking, 'Vhy dond't dey kom?'

The palace can claim at least three other ghost stories. One tells that the spectre of a 'man in breeches' is sometimes spotted wandering around the courtyard, and in 1912 Jessie Middleton recorded in her *The Grey Ghost Book* that the room in which Queen Mary II died of smallpox in 1694 was reputed to be haunted.

The third story concerns the ghost of Princess Sophia, fifth daughter of King George III (reigned 1760-1820). The tale is that Sophia fell in love with a royal equerry by the name of

Opposite above: *Kensington Palace.*

Opposite below: *The ageing King George II would spend long hours gazing at the weather vane.*

Right: *Statue of George II depicting him in Roman dress, in Golden Square, Soho.*

Thomas Garth and had an illegitimate son with him. The scandal was quickly hushed up and the child was taken from Sophia to be brought up elsewhere. Unable to bear the anguish, Sophia retreated from the world, taking solitary refuge inside her rooms at the palace. There she grew old, and unloved, she sat at her spinning wheel as the years passed, her eyesight failed and she gradually became blind. Sometimes, in the hushed hours of the early morning, the creaking of her spinning wheel can supposedly still be heard.

Built in the seventeenth century, Kensington Palace was originally a mansion known as Nottingham House until William III purchased it in 1689 and commissioned Sir Christopher Wren to oversee its enlargement. Although it continues to be a working palace and a residence for members of the Royal Family, parts of the building are now open to the public. Diana, Princess of Wales, lived in Kensington Palace until her death in 1997, as did Princess Margaret, who died in 2002. It is said that Princess Margaret was once asked whether she had ever seen the ghost of George II and replied that she had not, although she held out the hope of doing so one day.

Hyde Park

Hyde Park once echoed to the cries and thundering hooves of royal hunting parties. The Tudor king Henry VIII (reigned 1509-1547) seized this land from the monks of Westminster Abbey in 1536 and turned it into his private ground for hunting deer and wild boar. In the early seventeenth century, James I (king of England 1603-1625) granted limited public access to the park and it was fully opened to the public in 1637 during the reign of his successor Charles I

Above left: *Princess Sophia lies buried in London's Kensal Green Cemetery.*

Above right: *Statue of King Henry VIII at the main public entrance to St Bartholomew's Hospital.*

(reigned 1625-1649). Today, Hyde Park with its 350 acres and approximately 4,000 trees – not to mention its ghosts – is open to visitors all year round from 5 a.m. until midnight.

The park's best-known ghost story concerns a gnarled old elm known as 'Black Sally's Tree'. Sadly, this tree was lost to Dutch Elm Disease many years ago. It was probably one of the many large elms felled in Hyde Park during the 1970s but none of the park staff I asked in 2007 could say exactly where this particular tree used to stand. (I would be delighted to hear from any reader who does happen to know.)

Black Sally herself was apparently a vagrant who usually tramped the roads and fields between Bristol and Penzance but occasionally her wanderings took her into London. Tall and slim with Romany heritage, she had once been an attractive woman but now age and grime obscured her looks. It was that grime that gave her her name, for Black Sally boasted she had not washed her face for ten years, not since her husband had fallen in love with another woman, at which betrayal Sally left their home for the open road. She lived in constant terror that her husband would eventually track her down and kill her.

One day, Black Sally came to Hyde Park where she found herself drawn to a particular ancient elm. The other vagrants who slept in the park cautioned her against that tree, believing it to be haunted by something evil. At first Sally heeded their warnings but one night she lay down to sleep beneath its branches and in the morning she was found dead. For a vagrant to die in the park was not unusual and because there were no marks of violence upon her corpse the authorities put Sally's death down to natural causes. Some of the vagrants thought otherwise, however. They talked of having seen an unknown man lurking in the vicinity of the tree where she had died and they wondered if Black Sally's husband had at last found her. One vagrant told how for several nights after Sally's death, 'sighings and moanings' were heard coming from beneath the tree, and how a strange footprint could be seen on the ground there. At night that footprint was wet with blood, but the liquid mysteriously vanished by dawn and those who had known Black Sally well were able to recognise the footprint as her own.

The story of 'Black Sally's Tree' is one of many collected by the ghost hunter Elliott O'Donnell, who recorded it in his *Ghosts of London*. He gives no date for the events recounted but in that book, first published in 1933, he states that this story was narrated to him 'many years' before. O'Donnell spent numerous nights in Hyde Park during the years before the First World War, chatting to the vagrants who slept there and learning their superstitious tales, many of which were centred on the trees that were so important to these homeless men and women.

One uncomfortably warm night, O'Donnell was walking from the Marble Arch end of the park towards Lancaster Gate when he heard a terrible groaning that seemed to come from a nearby clump of trees. Thinking that someone needed help he looked to see who was there but could spot nobody. Not far away, though, several vagrants were sitting under another clump of trees and so he hurried across to tell them one of their companions was ill but to his surprise they showed no concern, merely replying that that spot was where a tramp known as 'Old Sammy' had died. His groans had often been heard there after his death, they said, which was why every vagrant familiar with the park knew better than to sleep there.

Another evening, a vagrant who claimed to have once been a churchman told O'Donnell about the moonlit night he had been walking in the north of Hyde Park, near the path that runs parallel with Bayswater Road. The park was gloomy and silent, and the man was deep in thought, his head bowed as he strolled across the grass. Then he glanced up to see a woman a few yards ahead of him walking in the same direction. He was struck by how shabby and frayed her clothing was and the way her heels showed through the splits in the backs of her boots. Wondering if she needed any help, the man walked faster to catch up with her but no matter how much he quickened his pace the woman always seemed to stay the same distance ahead.

Eventually they came to a point where several paths met, and there the man's attention was caught by a solitary tree standing black in the moonlight a short distance to his right. About 6 or 7ft above the ground, a sinister branch stretched out from the trunk. It bore an uncanny resemblance to a beckoning human arm and the long twigs at the end seemed to be bony fingers ready to clutch at anyone who strayed too close. Now the woman headed directly towards the tree and as she approached it the man realised for the first time that she appeared hazy and insubstantial. She walked into the tree's shadow and turned around – and the moonlight that now fell upon her face revealed that this was no living being, that whatever it was standing there in the form of a woman had been dead a long time. Horrified by the ghastly sight, the man fled from the park.

By the following evening, his fear had subsided and curiosity compelled him to return to search for the tree. He was certain he would recognise it by its striking appearance yet although he found the general area easily enough there was no trace of the tree itself and at last he asked an elderly man who knew the park better than anyone if he had ever seen a tree of that description. The old man seemed to know exactly what he meant and took him to a patch of open grass that he immediately recognised from the night before; this was definitely where the tree had stood but there was nothing there now. The tree had had a terrible reputation, the old man explained, because so many people had hanged themselves from its branches after sleeping beneath it and because so many rumours spoke of strange sights and sounds encountered in its vicinity at night. That was why the tree had been cut down – about twenty years before.

Left: *Many of Hyde Park's old ghost stories involved the trees that were so important to the vagrants living in the park.*

Below: *The north of Hyde Park; Bayswater Road is to the left in the picture.*

Another tree features in the tale of a vagrant known as All Button Mary, named for the great number of buttons she wore on her jacket. After sleeping beneath an elm she awoke in the morning to claim that a voice from the tree had whispered to her all night long, endlessly enticing her to kill herself and leave this miserable world for a better place. It seems that All Button Mary took the voice's advice for later that day her drowned body was discovered in the Serpentine.

The Serpentine dominates the southern end of Hyde Park. This artificial lake was created in the 1730s for Queen Caroline, wife of King George II, by damming the Westbourne Stream. At the time, artificial lakes were usually built long and straight and the Serpentine was one of the first in England deliberately designed to appear natural. It is a beautiful part of London but also one of those places that has acted like a magnet to the depressed and suicidal. One such person was Martha Sheppard, an unemployed maid who on the afternoon of Saturday 9 January 1858 climbed up onto the balustrade of the bridge over the Serpentine and leaped into the lake. Unfortunately for her (or fortunately, depending on your viewpoint), the large hooped crinoline skirt beneath her dress filled with air as she plummeted so that when she hit the water she simply bobbed around like a balloon for a few minutes until a policeman pulled her to safety. But many other suicide attempts were more successful. In the fourteen years leading up to 1858, for example, there had been 283 attempts in the Serpentine, ninety-one of which proved fatal.

It was in this same lake some decades earlier that the unhappy Harriet Westbrook Shelley drowned herself. Harriet was the first wife of the poet Percy Bysshe Shelley and had been abandoned by him for Mary Wollstonecraft Godwin (best known as the author of *Frankenstein*). She was just twenty-one years old when she took her life in 1816, out of wedlock and pregnant by a lover, and her ghost supposedly haunts these still waters. One story tells that two ladies walking through an almost deserted Hyde Park one blustery autumn day paused on the Serpentine's bank, looking into the lake where something was causing ripples to spread out. As they stood and watched, a slim pale hand – obviously a woman's – slid up from beneath the water's surface, the long fingers opening and closing convulsively like those of a drowning person. On the middle finger was a plain gold ring which flashed in the fading daylight. Too shocked to do anything but stare in horror, the ladies gazed at the sight for perhaps a minute, until at last the phantom hand slowly slipped back down and the waters closed over it.

The Serpentine has known murder, too. O'Donnell recorded that in 1857 a Newfoundland dog being taken for a walk near here suddenly raced away from its owners, plunged into the water and swam out towards a dark floating object which it seized and pulled back to the shore. It was the body of a murdered child. Following this gruesome discovery, rumours of ghostly activity beside the Serpentine apparently kept the lake's banks deserted after sunset for several weeks.

In the eighteenth century many duels were fought in Hyde Park, sometimes with fatal consequences, and perhaps one of these duels was responsible for the phantom sounds reported by a vagrant who often visited the park prior to the First World War. This man claimed that on several occasions as he slept beneath trees in the park he had been awakened by the ringing clash of metal on metal and an awful hollow groaning. It sounded, he said, as if two men were fighting with swords but the men were never seen.

One final spectral visitor is said to appear along Hyde Park's northern boundary, where a phantom horse-bus occasionally rattles along Bayswater Road. This supernatural vehicle appears perfectly solid and, so the story goes, most witnesses never even realise they have seen a ghost.

Bayswater Road is said to be haunted by a phantom horse-bus.

The Grenadier

It is the most famous haunted pub in London – and probably the world – but unless you're familiar with the area you may need a compass to find the Grenadier. Hiding in Belgravia's cobbled Wilton Row, it lies just a short distance south of restless Hyde Park Corner yet its atmosphere is that of a quiet country pub. A few narrow steps lead up to a small bar where, amid the military paraphernalia adorning the walls, a glass frame beside the bar protects yellowing newspaper cuttings that refer to the ghostly Guardsman said to haunt these premises.

If you hadn't already guessed by the name and interior décor, the bright red sentry box outside declares that this pub has military connections. The alley alongside is called Old Barrack Yard and it once echoed to the stamping, rattling and shouted orders of soldiers being drilled. The pub itself used to be named The Guardsman and an enduring myth holds that while the public once drank, gambled and brawled in a downstairs bar, the ground floor served as a mess for officers of the Duke of Wellington's Regiment. Tradition also maintains that the Iron Duke himself, whose home Apsley House stands nearby, occasionally visited the pub to drink and enjoy a hand of cards with his men but this seems unlikely for a man so ill-disposed towards drinking and gambling in public.

The story told as background to the haunting here states that a young subaltern was once caught cheating during a game of cards. His fellow officers, their better judgements impaired by alcohol, were so enraged that they seized him and brutally flogged him on the spot. So savage was his punishment that the subaltern staggered down the steps to what is now the cellar, where he collapsed and died. The year in which this is supposed to have happened is unknown, but it is said to have been in September, the month in which the disturbances at the Grenadier reach an annual peak.

Stories of strange happenings here were already well established by 1956, when Joseph Braddock recorded some in his book, *Haunted Houses*. The landlord then was Roy Grigg, who told Braddock that although he had some reservations about the truth of the cheating

The Serpentine.

officer story, he had little doubt that the pub was indeed haunted. There was, he said, a strange, menacing atmosphere here that underwent an annual cycle, building up throughout the year to climax in September. During the first two weeks of that month Grigg's young Alsatian dog always grew agitated, growling and snarling as if afraid. In the cellar it scratched away at the floor, apparently trying to unearth something and leading some to wonder if the subaltern's body was buried down there.

One September, or possibly October, evening in 1952, Grigg's son saw a mysterious black shadow. The nine-year-old boy was alone upstairs and as he lay in bed with the bedroom door open and the landing light blazing outside, a shadow appeared on the door. He watched in terror as the shadow grew larger and larger and then slowly shrank away, exactly as if somebody on the empty landing had walked towards the bedroom then changed their mind and retreated. That same year, Mrs Grigg was getting changed in her bedroom one afternoon and had not bothered to close the bedroom door because she knew she was alone on the top floor. She was shocked, therefore, to catch sight of a man coming up the stairs. Quickly covering herself she turned to see who it was and found … nobody. She had not recognised the man's face and she never saw him again.

A year later, a second person spotted an unknown man on the staircase. Mrs Ward, proprietor of a pub in Hammersmith, was drinking in the bar of the Grenadier when she clearly saw a man walking up the stairs, but no trace of the intruder was ever found. Also in 1953 a childhood friend of Roy Grigg was staying the night in one of the bedrooms after driving the Grigg family home from Plymouth. He had been warned by a barman that there was something untoward about the room and so, being a Roman Catholic, he hung a rosary over the bed for protection. Despite this precaution he awoke in the night to find the room icy cold and was uncomfortably certain he was not alone, that something was lurking in the darkness beside the bed, trying to touch him.

In 1966 Dr George Owen (a geneticist, biologist and mathematician) and the experienced journalist Victor Sims interviewed Geoffrey and Paula Bernerd who had by then taken over at the Grenadier. Owen and Sims wrote about the case in their 1971 book, *Science and the Spook*. 'When I first came to this place and heard all these ghostly tales,' Geoffrey Bernerd told them, 'I

The Grenadier, probably the most famous haunted pub in the world.

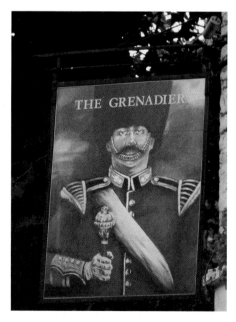

Above left: *Sign hanging over the Grenadier.*

Above right: *Old Barrack Yard.*

put them down to imagination and gossip. But now, I must admit, there's much more to them than meets the eye.' The Bernerds both stated that although nobody they knew had actually *seen* the famed phantom officer, staff members had certainly experienced plenty of mysterious happenings: light switches turning themselves off and on, footsteps being heard in empty rooms and pairs of socks apparently moving from one room to another. Some customers complained of a chilly atmosphere in a panelled back room. One particularly odd detail was, 'a tendency for beer bottle tops to fly off spontaneously in a horizontal direction.' Staff refused to sleep on the premises during September and some previous staff had left after claiming to see light bulbs unscrew themselves from their sockets and softly float to the ground and hear an electric buzzer sound with no one nearby to press it. It was even hinted that the phenomena affected some of the nearby houses in Wilton Row, where tapping sounds were heard and electric lights occasionally switched themselves off and on.

One day, head barman Tom Westwood was pulling a pint when the flow of beer suddenly shut off. He assumed that one of the glass pipes leading up from the barrels downstairs had snapped, an all-too frequent occurrence in cold weather and one that invariably resulted in a messy flood. He went down into the cellar expecting the worst but although the pipe had indeed snapped there was no leak because the tap on the barrel had been turned off. Nobody apart from Westwood had access to the cellar and he was unable to explain who could have turned off the tap.

On another occasion, the bar had closed for lunch and Westwood was sitting down for a meal with Mrs Miriam Hanson-Lester (Paula Bernerd's mother). All the ashtrays had previously been emptied and no fire was burning anywhere yet they both clearly saw a wisp of smoke appear in mid-air close to a shelf near the door. 'I thought at first that a customer had left a tab-end [cigarette butt] burning … ' stated Westwood '… but there seemed to be no source. It was rising from mid-air. Nothing was on fire and, as far as I could tell, no one was within yards of the spot. There seems to be no explanation and I have been puzzled ever since.' A few days later, a brewery inspector (a retired CID officer) was standing near the same spot when he suddenly felt a burning pain on his wrist. Examining his arm, Mrs Hanson-Lester found a mark there as if he had been burned with a lighted cigarette.

In a *Daily Express* article of 23 December 1967, after he had moved on from the Grenadier, Bernerd stated of the pub's resident ghost, 'He is always up to something. We hear loud, heavy footsteps coming from nowhere and loud, really loud, bangs on the doors when there is nothing there. Lights are turned on, things are thrown about.' He also reported that his teenaged daughter once saw what she described as a shadow that should not have been there, a description reminiscent of the mysterious shadow that terrified Grigg's young son. The same *Daily Express* article records that the then-current manageress, Greta Bouman, and her staff also knew of the Grenadier's ghostly resident and referred to it simply as HIM. Bouman's assistant, Valerie Roberts, recounted some of HIM's activities:

The other day the lounge door wouldn't open to any key. Then somebody came up and it was unlocked. Sometimes bottle tops spin *sideways* – not downwards – across the room. One Christmas I was in the lounge alone at 2 a.m. when I heard heavy footsteps above, from my bedroom. They went on and on. I was petrified.

Tom Westwood was succeeded as head barman by Greyam Fox, who took on the role from 1982 until 1983. Fox, too, experienced strange goings-on at the Grenadier, courtesy of the ghost which had by then become known as Cedric. Fox later described two events to Richard Jones of London Ghost Tours, which were published on that company's website (www.london-ghost-tour.com). At about 8.30 p.m. one winter's night, Fox went down to the cellar to fetch some cigars from the small wooden 'lock-up' where spirits and tobacco were stored. On busy nights such as this it was difficult to find time for a cigarette break and so Fox sometimes kept a cigarette handy in a glass ashtray in the 'lock-up'. Seizing the opportunity for a few moments' rest, he lit the cigarette and took a few crafty drags and as he did so the landlord's black cat wandered into the cellar. Abruptly, the temperature plummeted. The cat's instant reaction, either to the sudden cold or to some unknown factor, was to arch its back and sink its teeth and claws into Fox's leg. A moment later the ashtray shot from the shelf to Fox's left, and whizzed past his head to smash into the wall. Terrified, the head barman fled from the cellar.

Fox also recalled how one dark, wintry evening around the end of 1982 a photographer took some shots of the pub for an in-house magazine. A few weeks later, the photographer returned with the news that a strange image had shown up on one of the developed photographs. This particular shot had been taken from the restaurant entrance (to the right, seen from the front bar), looking towards the front window and the side door that leads out into Old Barrack Yard. Several photographs had been taken from this position but only one showed an indistinct image in one of the windowpanes. It looked a little like a face peering in, which was obviously impossible because, from the ground outside, that window is well above head height. The photographer thought that the image must be an illusion caused by shadows from the lantern and foliage hanging outside but when he blew up the image the 'face' became even more apparent. It appeared to belong to a young man wearing a fez-like hat and sporting a handlebar moustache.

In January 1988, Peter Martin arrived at the Grenadier as relief manager, taking over as manager in February 1990. The following year he was interviewed by John Spencer, co-author with Anne Spencer of *The Encyclopedia of Ghosts and Spirits*. Martin told Spencer that he remained sceptical of the claimed haunting but he also recounted how one time during his period as relief manager he had been at the bar with a friend of the then landlord. It was around midnight and the two men watched in amazement as a bottle rose several feet into the air and exploded.

He also revealed that keys had mysteriously gone missing on several occasions, only to turn up again later. In either 1988 or 1989, for example, he had needed the keys to the cellar to let in electricians to carry out some repair work. The keys were not in their usual place and when he eventually found them they would not open the lock. But when the same keys were handed to a friend of the electricians, the door yielded to him with no trouble whatsoever. The incident sounds remarkably similar to that reported by Valerie Roberts more than twenty years earlier.

No. 50 Berkeley Square

No. 50 Berkeley Square may be the most famous haunted house in the world. The terrifying tales told about this four-storey Georgian town house in the heart of fashionable Mayfair made it notorious throughout gas-lit Victorian London and its fame quickly spread. In 1907, Charles Harper wrote in *Haunted Houses* that this building, 'was long one of those things that no country cousin, come up from the provinces to London on sight-seeing bent, ever willingly missed'. Something awful was said to reside within a certain room on the top floor, something so horrific that it had quite literally scared people to death.

Built in 1740, the house has remained largely unaltered since it was last modernised more than a century ago, and the interior retains much of its eighteenth-century grandeur. It was the London home of George Canning – Prime Minister of Great Britain for four months from April to August 1827 – until his death at Chiswick on 8 August 1827, but the haunting here seems unrelated to

Right: *No. 50 Berkeley Square.*

Below: *How many of the office workers who enjoy their lunch each day in peaceful Berkeley Square Gardens know of No. 50's terrifying reputation?*

Statue of Prime Minister George Canning in Parliament Square.

that distinguished resident. It is not clear exactly when the house first acquired its evil reputation, although some believe that strange things started to happen soon after it was built, but by the early nineteenth century the house was often left unoccupied for long periods and doubtless the air of emptiness and neglect played a part in the ghostly stories that were by now being told.

In around 1840, neighbours complained of noises coming from the empty house. They occasionally heard footsteps and the sounds of heavy furniture or boxes being dragged across the floor, as well the jangling ring of the servants' bells. Eventually, one neighbour grew so fed up with the disturbances that he obtained a key to No. 50 and as soon as the ringing began he rushed into the house and down to the servants' area. There he found the bells still moving but the house itself deserted.

In August 1859, *Blackwood's Magazine* published a supernatural tale by Edward Bulwer-Lytton entitled *The Haunted and the Haunters; or, The House and the Brain.* (At the time of writing, this can be read on the Internet at, among other sites, www.gutenberg.org.) In his tale, Bulwer-Lytton described his haunted house as being 'on the north side of Oxford Street' but he is believed to have been thinking of the stories told of No. 50 Berkeley Square when he wrote it. In turn, his tale probably helped to inspire many more supposedly true stories about this building, and by the 1870s and 1880s the house's notoriety was at its peak.

The best known of all the stories tells of two sailors who found themselves fog-bound and penniless in London one night during the 1870s. Walking through Berkeley Square they saw a sign outside the obviously empty No. 50 stating that it was available to let and as they desperately needed shelter they broke in and settled down for the night in a room on the top floor. Hours later, they were woken from sleep by footsteps coming up the stairs. The steps – described in different accounts as slithering, muffled and hesitant, or heavy – came closer and closer to the sailors' room until at last they paused outside. Slowly, the door handle began to turn. What then entered the room has been called a shapeless and horrible something or alternatively a grotesque white-faced man with a gaping mouth; whatever it was terrified the two sailors so utterly that they panicked and tried to escape. Only one man made it out of the room, forced to abandon his companion as he pushed his way past the thing and fled down the stairs to safety. In one version of this story, he was discovered in the house the following morning, his sanity destroyed by whatever he had seen and his hair having turned white overnight. In another version, he rushed out onto the street where he encountered a policeman who accompanied him back to the house. Both versions end with the gruesome discovery of the second sailor's body impaled on the spiked railings below the top floor's middle window – the window of the haunted room. His neck was broken and in some accounts his dead face was twisted in a paroxysm of terror. Perhaps he fell out of the window in his desperate attempt to escape, or perhaps he jumped in terror rather than face the evil thing that had trapped him. He may even have been deliberately thrown to his death. Although it is unlikely that this incident ever actually occurred, the tale was widely believed at the time.

A second story is that of a family named Bentley who once moved into the house. As soon as they arrived, the younger of the family's two teenaged daughters began to complain of a disturbing, animal-like smell in the musty air. Her older sister was engaged to a young army captain named Kentfield and shortly after the Bentleys settled in, her fiancé arranged to visit for a few days. The night before Captain Kentfield's arrival, a maid preparing one of the upstairs rooms for him suddenly screamed. The household rushed up to find her collapsed on the floor, staring in horror at one empty corner and murmuring, 'Don't let *it* touch me.' She died in hospital the next morning, never revealing what she had seen, saying only that it was too horrible for words. When Captain Kentfield arrived later that day, the family told him what had happened and said that they would prepare a different room for him. But the solider insisted that he did not believe in ghosts and that he would stay in the allotted room despite the earlier tragedy. No more than half an hour after he retired for the night, the family heard Captain Kentfield scream and fire a single pistol shot. His dead body was found on the floor, still grasping the spent pistol and with his face contorted with fear. No trace was found of the bullet he had fired.

Other stories follow similar lines. A man who refused to listen to warnings not to sleep in the haunted room told his friends not to worry because he would ring the servants' bell if he needed help. If they heard the bell ring once, he told them, they were to ignore it because he might simply have grown nervous, but if it rang a second time then they should come to his aid. His friends continued to protest but he refused to listen and went to sleep in the room. At midnight his friends heard the bell ring. There was a pause – and then the bell rang again, more violently than before. They raced to the room, threw open the door and found their terror-stricken companion in the throes of a fit. He died shortly afterwards, never disclosing what had frightened him so much. Another tale says that the house was once let out to a couple of newly-weds. When their lease began they were still abroad on their honeymoon and so the wife's mother visited the house to ensure all was in readiness for their return. She had to travel a long way to reach London and by the time she arrived she was so tired she decided to go to bed early. At midnight, her screams awoke the servants and they ran to her aid, only to find her lying lifeless on the bed, her unseeing eyes wide open in an expression of horror. Then there is the tale of a man – a great sceptic on the matter of ghosts – who obtained permission to spend a night in the haunted room and took along as his sole companion, his faithful dog. Both were discovered dead in the room the following morning.

During the 1870s, Lord Lyttelton became so fascinated by the stories about No. 50 Berkeley Square that he arranged to spend a night on his own in the dreaded top-floor room to see what, if anything, might happen. Brave he might have been, but he was no fool and he wisely armed himself with a pair of blunderbusses, loading them with a mixture of buckshot and silver sixpences, the latter intended as a magical weapon against any evil forces that might assault him. During his lonely vigil that night, he was forced to grab one of his guns and fire at 'something' he was convinced had leaped out at him from the room's shadows. Whatever it was, he reported, fell to the floor 'like a rocket' but when morning arrived and light once more filled the room he could find no trace whatsoever of the thing he was certain he had shot.

The controversy surrounding the alleged haunting here provoked a lengthy correspondence in *Notes and Queries*, to which Lyttelton contributed. Whereas some correspondents suggested that the atmosphere of neglect and decay hanging over the empty house had inspired the many imaginative stories, Lyttelton believed that the haunting was itself the reason the house was so often left unoccupied. An 1879 article by W.E. Howlett in *Notes and Queries* neatly summarised the key elements of the stories told, 'The house in Berkeley Square contains at least one room of which the atmosphere is supernaturally fatal to body and mind [and rumours told of many cases] ending in death, madness or both as a result of sleeping, or trying to sleep in that room.' Howlett went on to write that the 'very party walls of the house, when touched, are found saturated with electric horror' and in 1881 a correspondent to *Notes and Queries* testified to the truth of this last claim. 'K.H.B' told of an incident that had taken place at No. 49 (next door to No. 50) during a society ball in 1880:

A lady and her partner were sitting against the party wall of No. 50 when on a sudden she moved from her place and looked round. The gentleman was just going to ask the reason when he felt impelled to do the same. On comparing their impressions, both had felt very cold, and had fancied some one was looking over their shoulders from the wall behind! From this it would appear that 'brick walls do not a prison make' for these uncomfortable ghosts, who can project themselves right through them to the great discomfort of their next-door neighbours.

According to Howlett's article, the house was in 1879:

... uninhabited save by an elderly man and his wife who act as caretakers; but even these have no access to *the* room. This is kept locked, the key being in the hands of a mysterious and seemingly nameless person who comes to the house once every six months, locks up the elderly couple in the basement, and then unlocks *the* room and occupies himself in it for hours.

More details of this intriguing tale were reported in the weekly magazine *Mayfair* on 10 May 1879:

In spite of the character of the house, some persons are occasionally found bold enough, or ignorant enough, to wish to become its tenants – but always in vain. A lady of high position lately made the attempt, and called at the house to make inquiries. It is popularly supposed that the house has no bodily inhabitants at all. But, after some delay, the door was opened by an old woman, who, holding the door in such a manner as to prevent any possibility of entrance, answered inquiries to this effect. The house was not to be let at all. She and her husband lived in it as caretakers. The landlord (unnamed by her) came once every six months; and then he would always lock the old couple up in one of the lower rooms, and went by himself into an upper room, which at other times was kept locked and of which he kept the key. And this was all that could be learned. Whether the upper room is *the* upper room is left to surmise, like what is done there; whether it is a chamber consecrated to magic by the rules of the black art, or whether it is used in some wiser or more innocent way.

Lord Lyttelton fired at 'something' that came at him from the shadows. (Anthony Wallis www.ant-wallis-illustration.co.uk)

By the 1890s, the stories about Mayfair's haunted house remained popular knowledge and debate rumbled on as to whether or not the tales were true, but No. 50's notoriety was fading. In his 1907 book, Charles Harper commented that although the building was still standing, it was 'no longer haunted, nor even empty. Years ago, it was indubitably unoccupied and sufficiently forlorn; but there are those who declare it was never haunted, and that the story was, indeed, invented by a more or less popular novelist of years ago.' (Presumably, he is referring here to Bulwer-Lytton's previously mentioned tale of 1859, believed to have fuelled many stories subsequently told about No. 50. Yet Bulwer-Lytton himself is supposed to have had No. 50 in mind when writing his tale, and so presumably at least some of the stories existed before he ever put pen to paper.)

But the saga was given a boost with the publication of a new book in 1912. In *The Grey Ghost Book*, Jessie A. Middleton wrote that she remembered hearing years before that the house was haunted by the ghost of a young girl wearing a 'Scotch plaid frock'. The girl had reportedly died in her nursery on the top floor, where she had 'been either tortured or frightened to death', and her 'pathetic little wraith, sobbing and wringing its hands, used to appear to the inmates until nobody dared to live in the house.'

In the 1920s the renowned psychic investigator Harry Price decided to investigate the tales of strange events at No. 50 Berkeley Square. Price was curious to know why this house, at such a desirable London address, had lain empty for so much of its history, and while he acknowledged that deserted houses naturally gathered odd rumours around them, he found this case suggestive of something stranger. He tended towards the opinion that beneath the accumulation of rumours and tall tales lay some genuinely mysterious phenomena, and he thought the cause might lie with poltergeist activity, centred not on an individual person (as in almost all reported poltergeist cases) but on the old house itself.

Many other theories have been advanced over the years. One was that the house was under a magical influence, the result of mysterious rituals performed on the first floor over many years by a lady who had once lived there. Another idea stated that the house was at some time in the late eighteenth century the headquarters of a gang of forgers and coin clippers who had encouraged tales of ghostly goings-on to keep people away and cover up any suspicious noises overheard by neighbours at night. In the late nineteenth century, some sceptics maintained that a caretaker had invented the stories to scare people from buying or renting the house and thus ensure that he or she could continue living there. A still popular theory for the origin of the stories concerns a Mr Myers who leased the house following the death of its previous occupant in 1859. Myers, a well-to-do man, was engaged to be married and spent all of his free time cheerfully redecorating the house for his bride-to-be. But in the best spirit of Victorian melodrama, he was jilted on his wedding day and the rejection utterly destroyed him. His heart broken, he went insane from grief, hiding from the world by locking himself in the top-floor room and admitting only his manservant to deliver his meals. He took to sleeping all day, temporarily emerging from his self-imposed exile at night to prowl around with a candle, gazing in misery at the fading grandeur of the happy life that should have been his. Rumours of the house being haunted are supposed to have been inspired by glimpses of the melancholic recluse rambling through his decaying home. Harper, in his 1907 book, offered another explanation, writing that the house had at one time belonged to a Mr Du Pré who imprisoned his lunatic brother in one of the attics. 'The captive was so violent,' wrote Harper, 'that he could only be fed through a hole. His groans and cries could be distinctly heard in the neighbouring houses.'

By the 1930s, it seems that the stories had once again died away, for in 1933 O'Donnell wrote in *Ghosts of London*, 'The original building may, or may not, I think, have harboured beings from another world, but whether it did or not, the present house … is absolutely free from any such phenomena.' Yet the story never completely faded. In 1969, Mrs Mary Balfour – then an elderly lady with a reputation for powers of clairvoyance – told a reporter about a ghost she saw in around 1937. She and her maid had moved south from the Scottish highlands and taken a flat in a road adjacent to Berkeley Square. She recalled:

> It was about the time of New Year, and I had come in late when my maid summoned me to the kitchen at the back of the flat. We could see into the back windows of a house diagonally opposite and in one of them stood a man in a silver-coloured coat and breeches of eighteenth-century cut, wearing a periwig and with a drawn, pale face. He was looking out sadly, not moving. […] It was only afterwards that I discovered that the house was number fifty. Believe it or not, I had not until that time heard of the reputation of the house.

Shortly after this, the building was leased to Maggs Brothers Ltd, the antiquarian booksellers who occupy the premises to this day. Because of the house's lingering reputation staff members are often asked if they have experienced any trouble with ghosts but for more than sixty years they have reported no unusual episodes at all. Recently, however, this may have changed. According to the 'London Walks' tours website (www.london-walks.co.uk), a cleaner preparing for a party in the building in 2001 had the uncomfortable feeling that something was standing behind her, and on a Saturday morning that same year, a member of staff was working alone in the haunted room when he was startled by a column of brown mist that swiftly crossed the room and then vanished. The website also reported that a man had his spectacles grabbed from his hand and thrown to the floor as he walked up the stairs. Perhaps the story of this celebrated but controversial haunting has not yet fully run its course …

CHAPTER TWO

ROYAL LONDON: AROUND THE GREEN PARK AND ST JAMES'S PARK

Buckingham Palace

Buckingham Palace has served as the British sovereign's official London home since July 1837 when Queen Victoria first took up residence here. It takes its name from Buckingham House, the town house bought by King George III for his wife, Queen Charlotte, in the 1760s and later substantially rebuilt. But legend speaks of an older building that once stood hereabouts, an ancient priory that vanished after the Dissolution of the Monasteries in the mid-sixteenth century, and of a monk whose ghostly shade continues to return to Buckingham Palace.

The story is that the monk died after being locked up in the priory's punishment cell for some long-forgotten transgression. His apparition, often said to wear a brown habit and to be bound in heavy, clanking chains, supposedly manifests briefly once every year, on Christmas Day, moaning miserably as it shuffles along the terrace overlooking the palace's 40 acres of gardens. Sadly for this tale, no priory or monastery ever existed on the site now occupied by the palace or its grounds. The Museum of London informed me in July 2006 that the nearest religious establishment to here was the leper hospital of St James, which stood on the site of the present-day St James's Palace (see 'St James's Palace, p. 37).

Perhaps the story of the ghostly monk originates from this hospital, for it and the surrounding land were once monastic property and the patients were originally cared for by monks, and then nuns to look after female patients. However, any record of who the unfortunate monk in the story might have been – if he ever existed at all – was almost certainly destroyed at the time of the Dissolution.

From within the walls of Buckingham Palace comes a second ghostly tale, this time from the early years of the twentieth century and concerning the sharp crack of a gunshot sometimes heard reverberating throughout the first-floor corridors. This is said to be the supernatural echo of the suicide of Major John Gwynne, private secretary in the household of King Edward VII (reigned 1901-1910), who became involved in a divorce case and, unable to cope with the scandal and public disgrace, shot himself in his office on the first floor.

Although this is a working palace housing many offices and frequently in use for great official events, areas of Buckingham Palace are regularly made open to the public and may be visited during August and September.

Above: *Buckingham Palace.*

Left: *Does a phantom monk haunt Buckingham Palace? (Jeremiah Deasey iStockphoto.com/upheaval)*

Opposite: *The Green Park offers a peaceful refuge from the busy city.*

The Green Park

The Green Park, which lies between Hyde Park and St James's Park, has a more subdued atmosphere than its often busy neighbours and this tranquil place offers a peaceful refuge from the city. Its ghosts seem to have faded away now but not so long ago there were many tales of supernatural beings haunting these grounds.

The first record of the park comes from 1554 and it was enclosed by Charles II a little more than a century later. Originally called Upper St James's Park, it had by 1746 become known as the Green Park. In years gone by duels were occasionally fought here and, as with Hyde Park (see 'Hyde Park', p. 11), there is a tale that the ghostly echo of one such fight can still be heard. On 11 January 1696, the chill air reverberated to the ring of clashing sword blades as Sir Henry Colt fought with Robert 'Beau' Fielding, a notorious rake and lover of the Duchess of Cleveland. The duel was fought in the vicinity of the Duchess's residence, Bridgewater House at the western end of Cleveland Row, and at its climax Sir Henry was run through, although not fatally. Each year, at dawn on the anniversary of the duel, the sounds of the struggle are supposedly replayed, drifting on the winter mist across the damp, icy grass. But perhaps this ghostly re-enactment has run its course. Mark Wasilewski is the park manager for both the Green Park and St James's Park, and he knows these parks well, having worked in them for many years, yet he told me in July 2006 that neither he nor his staff knew of any reports of this ghostly battle being heard, or had even been aware of this legend before.

Bridgewater House.

Several sinister tales were once told of trees in the Green Park and one tree in particular had a decidedly gloomy reputation. Sometimes referred to as the 'Tree of Death', it was apparently shunned by both humans and animals. People felt uneasy in its vicinity and a powerful aura of melancholy and grief emanating from it would overwhelm anyone who approached too close. It was said that several people had committed suicide by hanging themselves from the twisted, ancient branches, that children would not play nearby, birds would not land there and dogs would give the tree a wide berth. Walkers passing by who looked back uncomfortably, sensing they were being watched or followed, occasionally glimpsed a tall, darkly clad figure standing beside the gnarled trunk, staring at them – a figure that had mysteriously disappeared if they glanced back a second time. As with the legend of the ghostly duel, however, the current park staff are unaware of this story and could shed no light on where this tree stands, if indeed it still does. Yet the tree's black reputation was once very well known. In 1973, Peter Underwood recorded that he once talked to two park attendants who swore to him that they had heard various strange noises coming from it. There was the 'harsh and loud' sound of a male voice that would abruptly cease as soon as the listener became aware of it, as well as a sinister 'low and cunning' laugh and also the despairing sound of a soul in agony. As for why a tree should possess such an evil nature, some have speculated that it was somehow linked with the burial of lepers from the old leper hospital that stood on the site of St James's Palace. The theory is that, by some uncanny process, all the accumulated misery and pain of those wretched souls seeped from their remains into the earth, from whence it was taken up into the roots of the tree, absorbed, and incorporated into its very essence.

A ghostly duel is supposedly fought in the park near Bridgewater House.

Perhaps the story of the 'Tree of Death' is related to a tale from around the beginning of the twentieth century. In his *More Haunted Houses of London*, Elliott O'Donnell recalled how he was walking through the Green Park late one September night in either 1900 or 1901 when he heard the faint sounds of a distant fiddle. Curious as to who might be playing music at such a late hour, he followed the sounds and eventually decided that they came from a particular cluster of trees. He was heading for them when he chanced across a policeman and happened to remark that it was an odd time for a street musician to be playing. To his surprise, the policeman replied that O'Donnell could search all night without ever finding the fiddler and recounted a tale he had himself been told. Apparently, an aged fiddler had once gone to sleep beneath those trees and awoken to find that someone had stolen his fiddle during the night. He informed a policeman of the theft as soon as he could but the culprit was never caught and the fiddler sank into a deep depression at the loss of his livelihood. For the next few days he stayed around the trees without eating, stopping every passer-by to ask if they knew where his beloved fiddle might be but nobody could help him and eventually he tied his braces to a sturdy branch and hanged himself. Afterwards, many people heard music coming from those trees, especially around late September, and when the wind was blowing from the southwest, but only one person ever saw where the music came from. That was the policeman to whom the fiddler had originally reported the crime, who, the night after the fiddler's suicide, went to investigate the source of some music he heard and found the old fiddler sitting beneath the tree where he had died, playing for all he was worth.

Another tree was once known to some of the vagrants who frequented the Green Park as the Pig Tree. This was allegedly haunted by a terrifying apparition, whose pale, hate-filled eyes glared out from a hideous face described as pig-like but with a wolf's mouth and snout. The thing was hairless, lurid white and naked, with the body of a repulsive woman, and the story told was that on more than one occasion a vagrant had gone to sleep beneath that tree and died during the night, having been literally frightened to death. For some reason, only men were killed. Women, on the other hand, seemed strangely drawn towards the tree, although whatever presence inhabited its twisted branches exerted a malevolent influence that inspired in them a cruel hatred of the male sex.

Less sinister was the phantom reportedly seen by a man on a wet July afternoon shortly before the First World War. As he walked through the Green Park along a broad path running parallel with Piccadilly, a tall, grey-haired man caught up with and then passed him. The first man straightaway felt there was something odd about the other who despite the rain was without any hat or overcoat and was peculiarly dressed in evening clothes combined with a pair of dancing pumps. It also struck him that although his own footsteps made a quiet but distinct crunching sound as he walked across the damp path, the other man's movements were utterly silent. The figure continued walking ahead of him as they approached the intersection of several paths and he wondered which direction the man would choose. But as he watched, the figure became fainter and fainter and then faded away completely, leaving the man staring in bewilderment at the empty path ahead. This was supposedly the spirit of a man who had either shot or poisoned himself on a seat or bench in the Green Park some time around the beginning of the twentieth century.

Yet another old ghost story from this park concerned a certain seat reputedly haunted by a terrifying apparition: a crazed-eyed old man trying to cut his own throat with a broken razor. Fortunately, most people did not see this apparition directly but many who sat here had the uncomfortable feeling that something was glaring at them and as a result visitors to the Green Park learned to shun this seat. By 1920, the seat and its resident phantom had long since been removed, and today it seems that the Green Park's other ghostly inhabitants are also all long departed from this pleasant oasis of calm in the midst of London.

St James's Park

St James's Park is the oldest of London's Royal Parks and has undergone great changes over the centuries. Henry VIII acquired what was then swampy marshland in 1532 and turned it into a deer park. Later, Elizabeth I used the land as a setting for colourful fêtes and pageants. Drainage was significantly improved in the early seventeenth century and the park was extensively redesigned. In the early nineteenth century its appearance altered yet again when the great John Nash landscaped the grounds, essentially creating the park you can see today.

Centuries ago, a large pool known as Rosamond's Pond occupied the west end of the park, close to where Buckingham Palace now stands. This then pleasant and secluded locale was once a popular destination for romantic moonlit trysts but later gained a reputation as a suicide spot, favoured particularly by broken-hearted women. By 1770, the pond had been filled in but for many years afterwards the site of so much tragic despair was, unsurprisingly, rumoured to be haunted. Yet the area's best-known ghostly visitor died not by her own hand, but by someone else's.

Running along the park's south edge is a road named Birdcage Walk, at the western end of which stands Wellington Barracks, home to the British Army's five guards regiments: the Irish,

Birdcage Walk looking east; St James's Park is to the left.

Wellington Barracks.

Scots and Welsh Guards, the Coldstream Guards and the Grenadier Guards. It was here two centuries ago that several soldiers reported supernatural experiences and that two guardsmen were admitted to hospital suffering from what *The Times* described as 'the effects of fright'. So adamant were they about what they had seen that the Army held an inquiry into the matter, taking sworn statements from the witnesses.

At about 1.30 a.m., on or around 3 January 1804, George Jones of Lt-Col. Taylor's Company of Coldstream Guards 'perceived the figure of a woman without a head, rise from the earth at the distance of about two feet before me.' Jones was so 'alarmed' by this sudden appearance that he temporarily lost the power of speech and could only stare in wonder at the spectacle before him. During the two or so minutes before the apparition vanished, he 'distinctly observed that the figure was dressed in a red striped gown, with red spots between each stripe, and that part of the dress and figure appeared to me to be enveloped in a cloud.'

Another Guardsman, Richard Donkin of the 12th Company of Coldstream Guards, also had a strange experience at around the same date. He was on guard duty behind the Armoury House, when at around midnight he heard 'tremendous noise' from the windows of a nearby house which was supposed to be empty. At the same time, he heard a feeble voice crying out, 'Bring me a light! Bring me a light!' From the sound of the voice, Donkin concluded that somebody was ill and he called out an offer of help, which he repeated several times but every time he was greeted with the same faint call. He tried to see where the voice was coming from but could see nobody. And then:

> On a sudden the violent noise was renewed, which appeared to me to resemble sashes of windows lifted hastily up and down, but then they were moved in quick succession, and in different parts of the house nearly at the same time, so that it seems impossible to me that one person could accomplish the whole business.

Donkin concluded his statement by commenting that several other members of his regiment had reported hearing 'similar noises and proceedings', but no cause for them had ever been found. And it seems that odd encounters here are not restricted to soldiers. Civilians, too, have reported hearing strange noises after nightfall, sometimes describing the sounds as like running footsteps, and there have been glimpses of a figure in a light-coloured dress running in the direction of St James's Park. Peter Underwood (1973) told how one distraught driver reported almost knocking down a woman who ran across a road in the vicinity of the Cockpit Steps, a short distance to the east of Wellington Barracks. He described the woman as wearing a white dress seemingly spattered with blood, and said that the figure had appeared to be headless.

The ghost is popularly supposed to be that of a woman murdered by her husband near here in or around 1784. Her killer, a sergeant in the Coldstream Guards, cut off her head and disposed of the decapitated body by throwing it into the lake in St James's Park. However, as with the ghosts of the Green Park (see 'The Green Park', p. 29), tales of this phantom seem to have faded in recent years. When I contacted the Park Office in July 2006, Chloe Holloway told me that neither she, the park manager, nor any of the other staff members she questioned were aware of anyone claiming to have seen this ghost, or even of the ghost story at all.

As if one supernatural lady wandering these streets at night is not enough, there is also a story that the statue of Queen Anne sited in Queen Anne's Gate just to the south of the park sometimes comes to life! This apparently happens at the stroke of midnight on 1 August, the anniversary of the Queen's death in 1714, when the statue climbs down from its pedestal and walks three times back and forth along the street before returning to its place for another year.

Right: *At the top of the Cockpit Steps.*

Below: *Looking north from the bottom of the Cockpit Steps towards St James's Park.*

Above: *The lake in St James's Park.*

Left: *The statue of Queen Anne in Queen Anne's Gate is said to come to life once a year.*

St James's Palace

St James's Palace, just north of St James's Park, is reputedly haunted by one of London's grisliest ghosts, the spectre of a man whose throat has been slashed open.

The palace was built on the orders of Henry VIII on land once housing St James's hospital for lepers and it has played a central role in English history since. It was here that Anne Boleyn stayed the night after she was crowned queen, and that Mary Tudor signed the treaty surrendering Calais in 1558. When the Spanish Armada threatened her kingdom's shores, it was from St James's Palace that Elizabeth I rode out to address her troops. Following the destruction of the Palace of Whitehall in 1698, St James's became the main residence of successive kings and queens of England, and although Queen Victoria began a new tradition when she chose to live instead in Buckingham Palace (see 'Buckingham Palace', p. 27), it is St James's Palace that remains the official residence of the sovereign, which is why ambassadors from foreign powers are still formally accredited to the Court of St James.

A destructive fire in 1809 meant that much of the palace had to be rebuilt, but parts of the original red-brick structure remain, including the Tudor Gatehouse that stands at the southern end of St James's Street. Today, St James's is a busy working palace. It is not open to the public but it is well worth wandering along Marlborough Road and Cleveland Row to get a magnificent view of the palace exterior.

With so much history, it can come as no surprise that ghostly tales are told about this building, and one of these stems from an incident that took place in the early nineteenth century. Ernest Augustus (1771-1851), the Duke of Cumberland and fifth son of King George III, was not a man possessed of the 'common touch'. His boorish behaviour and general arrogance towards those around him made the duke one of the most unpopular men in London, and that unpopularity deepened to hatred after the mysterious death of his valet, a little Sardinian named Joseph Sellis.

On the night of 30-31 May 1810, Ernest returned to his rooms within the palace late after spending the evening at a charity performance of Handel's *Messiah*. The events that followed have recently been dealt with at length by John Wardroper in *Wicked Ernest* (2002) and are the subject of much controversy. According to Ernest's own sworn deposition he retired to his four-poster bed and went to sleep, only to be awoken by two blows to his head. Still half asleep he felt another two blows and, so he claimed, it occurred to him that a bat had flown against him. Despite the lamp burning in his room Ernest apparently caught no glimpse of his attacker as he struggled to reach an adjoining door leading to the room where one of his valets, a man named Cornelius Neale, lay sleeping. (In some accounts of the story, Neale is named as Yew or Yeo.) Now a sword blade cut into his right thigh yet still Ernest restrained himself from retaliating, instead calling out to Neale that there was a murderer in his room. For some reason, this call for help frightened the unknown assailant who ran off through a second door (which should have been locked but for some reason wasn't), fleeing, 'through the yellow room which leads into the ballroom, through the other yellow room into the armoury, to the summer bedroom, through the dressing-room into Sellis's room'.

Cornelius Neale's version of events supported Ernest's. Although Neale described himself as a light sleeper and his room was separated from Ernest's 'only by a thin ... wainscot partition', he said that he heard no sound of any struggle until the wounded Ernest opened his door, crying, 'Neale! I am murdered!' Neale hurried into the duke's room where he found a bloodstained sword and wanted to 'pursue the assassin' but Ernest told him to first wake up the other servants and then accompany him to the porter's lodge to raise the alarm. After this had been done they

Above: *St James's Palace, seen from Marlborough Road.*

Left: *St James's Palace; the gatehouse at the southern end of St James's Street.*

returned to the duke's bedroom and Ernest instructed Neale to find out where the attacker had concealed himself. It did not take Neale long. Inside a closet, he said, he discovered a scabbard, a water bottle and a lantern, along with an incriminating pair of slippers with the name Sellis conveniently written in them.

Joseph Sellis's bedroom was located about 100ft to the east of Ernest's and it was in there that his corpse was now discovered, lying on his bed. It was clear at once that he was dead. His throat had been slashed from ear to ear so savagely that the head was almost severed from the body, and the bed and bedclothes were drenched in blood. More blood was smeared on the doors and frames between Sellis's room and Ernest's. On the floor near the body was a cut-throat razor and on the opposite side of the room was a partially filled hand-basin, in which someone had apparently tried to wash away blood.

The duke gave his explanation for what must have happened: Sellis had obviously tried to assassinate him, inflicting serious injury on him before escaping back to his room where, aghast at what he had done, he took his own life. An inquest was duly held where, perhaps because of Ernest's position, this version of events was readily accepted as the truth and the verdict passed was that Sellis had committed suicide. Cumberland was officially declared an innocent man. He would later travel to continental Europe to fight in the wars against Napoleon and in 1837 would become King of Hanover.

Yet doubt has always tainted both the verdict and Ernest's testimony. Key witnesses were not called to give evidence at the inquest and many important questions were never satisfactorily answered. Why, for example, would an assassin hide in a closet with a pair of slippers bearing his own name? And why, faced with his defenceless, wounded target, would the attacker throw down his weapon and run away back to his own room? It was also clear very early on that Ernest's wounds were by no means as serious as he had suggested. Sir Henry Halford, the royal physician, who helped treat the duke after the incident, concluded that there was 'no danger to the Duke of Cumberland's life', calling the situation a 'most providential escape'. Indeed, it is difficult to believe that a sabre-wielding would-be assassin faced with a sleeping target could manage to inflict so little harm and some have wondered whether the duke's rather superficial injuries were actually self-inflicted, intended to disguise the real events of that night.

Despite the verdict and the efforts made to draw a veil over the matter, the London public were only too ready to believe that Ernest had murdered Sellis and rumours and gossip spread. Amongst the stories were claims that the duke had seduced Sellis's daughter (possibly making her pregnant) and Sellis had discovered the truth, or that Sellis had caught the duke in bed with Mrs Sellis. Many people came to believe that Sellis had been about to reveal some unsavoury secret about Ernest's private life, a scandal perhaps involving sexual practices of a shockingly perverse nature. Faced with the impending revelation, they wondered, had Ernest – perhaps with the aid of Neale – silenced Sellis by slashing his throat, inventing the story of an attempted assassination to cover up the foul deed?

Such rumours refused to go away and the vilified duke eventually sought refuge abroad. Even then, stories continued to circulate about the mysterious death and the suspicion of unpunished murder. History has tended to dismiss the many scandalous tales told about the Duke of Cumberland but, according to evidence presented by Wardoper, there is reason to suspect Ernest was indeed involved in Sellis's death. Captain Charles Jones had served as Ernest's aide-de-camp during the wars against Napoleon. The two men liked and respected one another and Ernest appears to have trusted Jones enough to unburden himself of a great secret. A little before midnight on Christmas Eve 1815, Ernest's guilty conscience drove him to make what Jones later described as the 'dreadful confession':

Swear to me, my dear Jones, that you will never divulge what I am going to say to you, for my mind requires relief. […] You know that miserable business of Sellis's, that wretch, I was forced to destroy him in self defence, the villain threatened to propagate a report & I had no alternative.

The unfortunate Sellis was ignominiously buried according to the prescribed rules for suicides, at the dead of night, with no Christian obsequies, at a place where three roads met: a 'three-went way'. He was buried in secrecy for fear of crowds gathering and causing trouble, 'midway between the bottom of Northumberland-street and the gateway into Scotland Yard'. The scene has changed much since and his body lies near what is now the Sherlock Holmes public house at the junction of Northumberland Street and Northumberland Avenue. The corpse had a stake driven through it bearing Sellis's initials, yet this precaution does not seem to have kept his restless spirit from wandering.

The gruesome apparition of Joseph Sellis is said to haunt St James's Palace still, appearing in the room where he died, his blood-drenched body lying on the bed just as it was discovered in 1810, with a hideous gash in his throat and his mouth hanging open in a terrible, silent scream. It is sometimes claimed that the spectre appears on the anniversary of that terrible night. Others maintain that the echoes of muffled shouts and a violent struggle are occasionally heard, and that the horrific phantom wanders the palace corridors, spreading the sickly sweet stench of blood throughout this historic building.

The other supernatural tale emanating from St James's Palace is even older. During the seventeenth century, certain suites of apartments here were home to two ladies who had achieved considerable notoriety in the courts of King Charles II (reigned 1660-1685) and Charles's brother and successor, King James II (reigned 1685-1688). Hortense Mancini, the Duchess of Mazarin, had been one of Charles's mistresses but now she and Madame de Beauclair, once loved by James, found themselves passed over in favour of younger ladies and as the pair lived out their later years in their rooms at the palace their shared experience of fading glory forged a deep bond of companionship between them. Their conversations were many and varied but one topic to which they often returned was the possibility of some manner of continued existence after the death of their earthly bodies. One day they made a solemn compact that the first of them to depart this life would endeavour to return to this world to communicate with the other.

The first of the ladies to pass on was the Duchess of Mazarin, and as she lay dying the friends reaffirmed the promise they had made to each other. Yet afterwards the weeks and months and then the years passed with no sign of any message from the other side. Whatever faith Madame de Beauclair had possessed in the immortality of the soul was eaten away by her ever-deepening disappointment and she grew coldly sceptical, declaring finally and bitterly that there was no life after death. When she eventually died, she now knew, that would truly be the end of her.

Some months after this declaration, a friend of de Beauclair's received a message, imploring her to come at once to the palace if she wished to see her friend alive. This lady at first hesitated as she was herself feeling rather unwell, suffering from a nasty cold, but then a second, even more urgent-sounding message was delivered, begging the lady's attendance at the palace. Worried, she left in the company of a gentleman friend who later recorded the events of that night.

When they arrived, fully expecting Madame de Beauclair to be on her deathbed, they were astonished to find her in seemingly good health. Nevertheless, de Beauclair assured them that she would in a very short while be departing this life to enter that eternal realm, the existence of which she had admittedly come to deny but which she now knew to be real. Her conversion had come about, she revealed, after she had at last received a visit from the shade of her long-

Right: *The gruesome apparition of Joseph Sellis is said to appear in the room where his blood-drenched body was discovered. (Anthony Wallis www.ant-wallis-illustration.co.uk)*

Below: *Joseph Sellis was buried at a 'three-went way' close to where the Sherlock Holmes pub now stands.*

departed friend, the Duchess of Mazarin. Madame de Beauclair's statement was reproduced by T.M. Jarvis in his *Accredited Ghost Stories* (1823):

> I perceived not how she entered, but turning my eyes towards yonder corner of the room, I saw her stand in the same form and habit she was accustomed to appear in when living: fain would I have spoken, but had not the power of utterance. She took a little circuit round the chamber, seeming rather to swim than walk, then stopped by the side of that Indian chest, and, looking on me with her usual sweetness, said, 'Beauclair, between the hours of twelve and one this night you will be with me.' The surprise I was in at first being a little abated, I began to ask some questions concerning that future world I was so soon to visit; but on the opening of my lips for that purpose, she vanished from my sight.

The midnight hour was already almost upon them and still Madame de Beauclair showed no sign of any illness whatsoever and her guests attempted to cheer her up. But almost as soon as they began to speak, de Beauclair suddenly exclaimed, 'Oh! I am sick at heart' and collapsed.

One of those present at the scene 'applied some restoratives' to the stricken lady but it was no use. Within half an hour Madame de Beauclair was dead, having passed on at precisely the time her ghostly visitor had foretold.

Clarence House

Clarence House, adjoining St James's Palace, was built in 1825 for the Duke of Clarence before his accession to the throne as King William IV (reigned 1830-1837). Today it is the official residence of Their Royal Highnesses, the Prince of Wales and the Duchess of Cornwall.

During the Second World War, the building housed the offices of the British Red Cross Society's Foreign Relations Department and among the clerks working here then was a young woman named Sonia. Years later, she wrote to author Joan Forman to recount a frightening encounter she had here in the 1940s, when she was eighteen or nineteen years old. The punishing wartime work schedule demanded that clerks worked more than fifty hours each week, which would normally have included Saturday afternoons; however, the staff had learned to arrive early in the mornings, cut short their lunch breaks, work a little longer in the afternoons and generally store up enough time so that every now and again they could have a free Saturday afternoon to relax and recharge themselves. Unfortunately, Sonia had been unable to resist a couple of social engagements one week and now found herself forced to put in the necessary hours one miserable afternoon on a damp Saturday in late October or early November. Her colleagues had gone home and she was left sitting alone in her first floor office, at her desk with piles of paper and a typewriter. Elsewhere in the building she could hear the faint sounds of doors opening and closing, apparently in the vicinity of the ballroom. This puzzled her a little, for she had thought she was the only person working late that day, but she persuaded herself it must be the caretaker and thought nothing more of it.

Time dragged by as she slowly ploughed her way through her work but after a while she began to be bothered by a nagging sense that she was not alone in the room, that someone was lurking just out of sight, watching her. It's just your imagination, she told herself, but the feeling would not go away. At last, she turned around to set her mind at rest, knowing she would see nothing but the empty room. Instead, she was greeted by a sight that terrified her, a bizarre apparition she described as, 'a sort of greyish, swirling, triangular, smoky mass, oddly without

Clarence House.

feet – bobbing, receding and advancing alternately.' She leapt out of her seat, knocking her shin against an open filing cabinet drawer as she did so, grabbed her coat and fled. As frightened as she was, she remembered to pull the blackout curtains closed and with the room now even darker she raced down the stairs and out into the courtyard, still struggling to get into her coat, and hurried to the safety of her own home.

Upon her return to work on the Monday, she told her colleagues what she had seen and one remarked, 'It was probably the old Duke of Connaught.' Arthur, Duke of Connaught and Strathearn, was the third son of Queen Victoria, and had used Clarence House as his London residence since 1900. He died on 16 January 1942 at Bagshot Park in Surrey, aged ninety-one. Perhaps Sonia's encounter, the precise year of which she had long forgotten, had happened a few months after the duke's death and that was what prompted her colleague's remark, or perhaps there had already been some story that the duke's ghost haunted the building. Unfortunately, Sonia, who had spent a decade of her young life living in Soviet Russia, did not know who the Duke of Connaught was and did not pursue the remark and so we will probably never know.

It is possible to visit Clarence House by joining a guided tour, but only if you book your ticket in advance. Further information is available at www.royalcollection.org.uk.

CHAPTER THREE

WESTMINSTER: POLITICIANS AND PRIESTS

No. 10 Downing Street

The famous black door of No. 10 Downing Street opens into the core of British government. Here is the office of the British Prime Minister and the room where the Cabinet meet, as well as numerous other offices scattered around various floors for the many staff whose job it is to support the Prime Minister. The address is also a venue for official functions as well as the traditional home for the Prime Minister's family, in the private flat on the second floor. It is an extremely busy place yet it seems there is also room for a generous complement of ghosts.

Traces of Roman and Saxon buildings have been found within the grounds of No. 10 but the earliest building known to have stood where Downing Street is today was the Axe Brewery which was owned by the Abbey of Abingdon during the Middle Ages. The first domestic house recorded on the site of No. 10 was a building leased to Thomas Knyvet by Elizabeth I in 1581. Knyvet was later knighted and is best remembered today for arresting Guy Fawkes and foiling the Gunpowder Plot of 1605. In the 1620s Knyvet House (as it had become) was passed on to Sir Thomas's niece, Elizabeth Hampden, and became Hampden House. This was acquired in 1682 by the scheming Sir George Downing, a man described by the diarist Samuel Pepys as, 'a perfidious rogue', to whom property development was all about profit. Downing pulled down the existing buildings and replaced them with a cul-de-sac of between fifteen and twenty cheaply built terraced houses along the north side of the street. The numbering was very different to what we see now: No. 10 was originally No. 5 and was not renumbered until 1779. Interestingly, the present No. 10 is more than it appears to be as it is actually two houses joined together. Downing's terraced house stands at the front but inside the house is joined to a much grander building that dates from around 1677 and overlooks Horse Guards Parade.

The association between No. 10 and the Prime Minister began in the 1730s. Great changes were underway in Britain during the early eighteenth century as rule by the monarchy gave way to a new Parliamentary style of government. Sir Robert Walpole – 'First Lord of the Treasury' and effectively Britain's first Prime Minister – was given both the house on Downing Street and that overlooking Horse Guards by King George II as a grand residence befitting this new type of leader and Walpole took up residence in 1735 after having the two houses joined together. But Walpole refused to accept the property as a personal gift, insisting that it be made available to his successors. Some of Walpole's successors chose to live here while others did not, but

Above left: *The entrance to Downing Street.*

Above right: *The mysterious aroma of cigar smoke has been linked with Sir Winston Churchill; this shows the statue in Parliament Square.*

since the time of Prime Minister Arthur Balfour (in office from 1902–1905) No. 10 Downing Street has been the traditional residence and office of all British Prime Ministers in their role as First Lord of the Treasury.

One resident who seems to have stayed much longer than expected is a man dressed in the fashion of the Regency period. His ghost is said to appear in the garden and perhaps inside the house too, and it was reportedly seen by workmen in around 1960 as they carried out building work at No. 10. Some say that this is the ghost of a former Prime Minister and that he appears at times of national crisis. The Regency lasted from 1811 until 1820, which makes one wonder whether the ghost might be that of Spencer Perceval, a cold and unfriendly man who became Prime Minister in 1809 and is the only British Prime Minister to have been assassinated. As he walked into the lobby of the House of Commons late in the afternoon of 11 May 1812, he was shot in the chest by a man named John Bellingham (see 'The Houses of Parliament', p. 47). Perceval's body was taken back to No. 10 and lay there for five days before his funeral.

The building's other phantoms include the apparition of a tall, top-hatted gentleman who walks into the entrance lobby and straight out through the (closed) front door, and the sound of mysterious footsteps that have been reported by people in the garden and by policemen on guard duty.

Another ghostly resident is known as 'The Lady'. She has been seen by several messengers as well as by staff working in offices close to the Pillared Drawing Room, the magnificent room named after its striking Ionic columns that 'The Lady' is said to haunt. She is described as wearing a long dress and a fine set of pearls.

From the basement come stories of people who, as they wandered the subterranean corridors, have felt a young girl take hold of their hand.

Also in the basement, several people have reported a mysterious odour that manifests from time to time – the strong and distinctive smell of cigar smoke. This has, of course, been linked with Britain's cigar-smoking wartime Prime Minister, Winston Churchill. And it was Churchill who one night experienced a life-saving presentiment inside No. 10. It happened during the Blitz, on 14 October 1940, as he dined in the Garden Rooms, the only area of No. 10 to be reinforced against the German bombs. Several loud explosions nearby were followed by a near miss when a bomb fell on Horse Guards Parade, only about a hundred yards away. Suddenly, Churchill had a strong feeling concerning the large plate-glass window in the kitchen. 'I got up abruptly,' he recorded in *Their Finest Hour* (1949), 'went into the kitchen, told the butler to put the dinner on the hot plate in the dining-room, and ordered the cook and the other servants into the shelter, such as it was.' Just minutes later, the building was shaken by a violent crash as a large bomb hit Treasury Green fifty yards away, destroying the Treasury shelter, killing three civil servants and, as Churchill had seemingly predicted, shattering the kitchens in No. 10.

The Houses of Parliament

The Houses of Parliament are also known as the Palace of Westminster and a royal palace may have existed on this site as far back as the days of King Cnut (or Canute, reigned 1016-1035). The area has been associated with the institutions of government since the Middle Ages although the imposing complex of Gothic Revival buildings that stands today dates back only as far as the middle of the nineteenth century. A disastrous fire in October 1834 destroyed almost all of the Old Palace, after which rebuilding began in 1840 and the new Houses of Parliament were formally opened in 1852.

Since then, the 316ft-tall clock tower overlooking Westminster Bridge has been one of London's most recognisable symbols, even if many people get its name wrong. The correct title is St Stephen's Tower, and not 'Big Ben' as is often thought; the latter is the nickname of the massive Great Bell that chimes within the tower. Two stories seek to explain the origin of this odd nickname. The first is that the bell, which weighs over 13 tonnes, was named after Ben Caunt, a champion heavyweight boxer of the period. The second, more likely, explanation is that the name refers to Sir Benjamin Hall, First Commissioner of Works from 1855 to 1858, whose name is actually inscribed on the bell. Big Ben's chimes feature in a curious tale of prophecy from 1861, recorded in Chambers's *Book of Days*. On Thursday 14 March that year:

> ... the inhabitants of the metropolis were roused by repeated strokes of the new great bell of Westminster, and most persons supposed it was for a death in the royal family. It proved, however, to be due to some derangement of the clock, for at four and five o'clock, ten or twelve strokes were struck instead of the proper number.

By a curious coincidence the superstition that the great bell striking out of order portended a royal death was borne out on this occasion for it was later announced that the Duchess of Kent (Queen Victoria's mother) was close to death, and she did in fact pass away on 16 March.

In the palace itself, the Members' Lobby in the House of Commons is the site of the only assassination of a British Prime Minister and from this event comes a second tale of prophecy. In May 1812, a Cornishman by the name of John Williams reportedly experienced a vivid dream

Above: *The Houses of Parliament.*

Left: *'Big Ben' is housed within St Stephen's Tower.*

in which he found himself sitting in the Members' Lobby looking at a man wearing a blue coat and white waistcoat. As Williams watched, a second man dressed in a dark coat with distinctive buttons produced a pistol and shot the first, who fell to the ground with blood pouring from a wound in his chest. The drama startled Williams into wakefulness and he told his wife what he had dreamed before going back to sleep and experiencing the same dream for a second time. The next day he was so disturbed that he recounted his dream to some friends who found it all highly amusing. But a few days later news reached Cornwall that Prime Minister Spencer Perceval had been shot and killed in the Members' Lobby by John Bellingham, a man who had been imprisoned in Russia under dubious circumstances and was angry with the British Government for not compensating him. When Williams later saw an artist's impression of the incident he recognised the assassin immediately for the man portrayed was wearing exactly the same coat he had seen in his dreams.

Spencer Perceval's ghost possibly appears from time to time in nearby Downing Street, (see 'No. 10 Downing Street', p. 45) but he does not seem to haunt the site of his death. In fact, the Palace of Westminster does not appear to house a single ghost in the traditional sense of that word, although there is a remarkable story from 1905 concerning the phantom of a living person.

It was shortly before Easter that year, and Major Sir Frederick Carne Rasch – Unionist Member of Parliament representing the Chelmsford Division of Mid-Essex – was suffering from influenza. He had become quite seriously ill, yet this dedicated man was determined to continue with his Parliamentary duties. The evening before Parliament rose for the Easter holidays, the popular novelist and MP Sir Gilbert Parker was attending a Parliamentary debate where he was concerned to see Sir Carne Rasch, a friend of his, seated nearby and looking terribly ill. As the front page of the *Daily Express* of 12 May 1905 described the sight, Sir Carne Rasch was, 'deadly pale; his eyes closed, as if in approaching sleep; his chin was sunk between his hunched-up shoulders. He sat in a profound silence.' Sir Gilbert was certain of the figure's identity because they were sitting, as the *Daily Express* put it, 'only one bench and an angle apart' and he described his friend's appearance in the following terms, 'His face was remarkably pallid. His expression was steely. It was altogether a stony presentment – grim, almost resentful'. But he had little time to study the figure because a moment later Sir Carne Rasch was no longer there. There was no feasible way he could have stood up and walked away without being seen. He had simply vanished.

Sir Gilbert reported afterwards:

> That puzzled me and I at once went in search of him. I expected, in fact, to overtake him in the Lobby. But Rasch was not there. No one had seen him. I tried both the Whips and the door-keeper, equally without avail. No one had seen Sir Carne Rasch. I went round the House, inquiring in all the corridors and to the same end – Sir Carne Rasch had not been seen. Going again to the Lobby, I heard that Sir Henry Meysey-Thompson, who was at the Lobby post-office, had also been inquiring for the major, but without result. I joined Sir Henry, and we exchanged views.

Sir Gilbert, knowing something of the concepts of theosophy and the astral plane, wondered whether what he had seen was the spirit of the dead or dying Sir Carne Rasch. Sir Henry (who had not seen the figure but had gone to the post office to inquire after Sir Carne Rasch because he wanted to talk to him about some Parliamentary matter) was impressed by Sir Gilbert's account and the two men made a note of the date and time of the event. Several days later, Sir Carne Rasch met with Sir Gilbert and Sir Henry and heard their story. With a stolid good humour he accepted their congratulations upon not having died and he later made light of the episode in an address to his constituents at Great Leigh, near Braintree in Essex, on Saturday 13 May:

> Ghosts are generally supposed to be the apparitions of the dead, aren't they?
>
> I was rather ill at the time and had to keep my bed, and why I should have gone up to the House of Commons that night I don't know. However, the *Express* of Friday says that I did. I am worth a good many dead ones yet, I hope. At any rate, I mean to go on a little longer.
>
> I feel, however, that I ought to apologise to the Liberal party for not having died when I suppose I ought. Had I done so, it would have saved them a good deal of trouble. If I have another chance, perhaps I will endeavour to oblige them.

Not everybody was convinced that this was a genuinely paranormal event, however. Miss Alice Johnson, secretary of the Society for Psychical Research offered the suggestion of 'mistaken identity'. Perhaps, she wondered, Sir Gilbert had been dwelling on his friend's illness and it was this preoccupation that caused him to momentarily 'see' Sir Carne Rasch at the debate. Sir Gilbert, meanwhile, was troubled by the experience and did wonder whether he might have been mistaken. Sir Carne Rasch himself, on the other hand, appeared to be quite ready to believe that his inner conflict between the desire to perform his duties and the physical need to retire to bed had 'precipitated' his spirit form, which had attended the debate in his place. Perhaps Sir Gilbert had not been mistaken after all, for on 17 May a letter was published on page seven of the *Daily News*, in which Sir Arthur Hayter offered supporting testimony as to the reality of the incident:

> I beg to say that I not only saw Sir Carne Rasch myself sitting below the gangway (not in his usual seat), but that I called the attention of Sir Henry Campbell-Bannerman to whom I was talking on the Front Opposition Bench, saying that I wondered why all the papers inserted notices of Sir Carne Rasch's illness, while he was sitting opposite apparently quite well. Sir Henry replied that he hoped his illness was not catching.

Sir Carne Rasch wrote to the *Daily News* to bring the matter to a conclusion and in his letter published on 18 May 1905 headed 'Astral Politics', he jokingly stated:

> I certainly was not in my place at Westminster at the time, and had I been seen by other than hon. members (for whom I have, of course, the most profound respect) I should say they had 'got 'em again.' As it is, the tale wants finish. I ought to have done what was expected of me—and I must try to remedy this on a future occasion.

In fact, Sir Carne Rasch lived for another nine years, dying on 27 September 1914 at the age of sixty-six.

Another strange story featuring a spectral double or doppelganger concerns a member of staff named Mr Milman and his wife, both of whom are said to have lived in the Palace of Westminster for a number of years during the 1920s. Apparently, a doppelganger of Mrs Milman caused great confusion for several months. Her double appeared perfectly solid and was almost identical to her except that it never spoke to anyone and seemed to delight in mischief. For example, it would go around opening doors that Mrs Milman had recently locked. The existence of this doppelganger was first realised when a House Steward, having

Westminster Abbey.

just seen (he believed) Mrs Milman walking around on the ground floor, found her just a few moments later resting in an upstairs room. The Parliamentary Archives do not hold many records of previous staff and the only Milman listed in their catalogue is Sir Archibald Milman, who was Clerk Assistant of the House of Commons from 1886 to 1900 and then Clerk of the House of Commons from 1900 to 1902, and who lived in the Palace of Westminster for a fair amount of his life. Perhaps Sir Archibald was the 'Mr Milman' referred to in the story but the dates given argue against this because Sir Archibald died in 1902. (I am grateful to assistant archivist Jennie Lynch from the House of Lords Record Office for these archive details.)

Readers wishing to tour the Palace of Westminster should see the United Kingdom Parliament website at www.parliament.uk for details of how to arrange a visit.

Westminster Abbey

The Gothic splendour of Westminster Abbey stands on what was once known as Thornea, or Thorney Island. Measuring around 470 yards by 370 yards, this small island would likely have been a low, flat sandbank, thickly covered with unwelcoming brambles, around which two arms of the lost Tyburn stream flowed into the River Thames.

Statue of St Peter, St Peter's Square, Rome. (JCOLL–FOTOLIA)

The site's early history is lost in legend. There are claims that a church has stood here since the second century AD and that a pagan temple to Apollo once stood on the same ground, but such stories may well have been invented by early monks to enhance the Abbey's prestige. One doubtful tale attributes the founding of a church here to Saberht (also spelled as Saebert, Saeberht or Sebert), the first Christian king of the East Saxons (Essex), who reigned between around AD 604 and AD 616, and it is to the construction of this building that the following legend refers.

The night before the church was to be consecrated, a poor fisherman was out in his boat on the Thames when a stranger called to him from the Lambeth shore. The stranger – an elderly man in monk's clothing – persuaded the fisherman to ferry him across the river to Thorney Island and when they reached the island he asked the fisherman to wait for him as he headed off through the brambles towards the new church. A short while later, the dark night was illuminated by a dazzling celestial glow and the air trembled to the terrible beauty of angelic singing. When the stranger returned, he asked the awestruck fisherman to ferry him back across the river and only then did he reveal his true identity, that he was none other than St Peter and that he had visited the site to personally consecrate the new church. The saint bade the fisherman go to Mellitus – the Bishop of London – the next day to tell what he had witnessed. He also caused the fisherman to catch an enormous haul of good salmon, saying that one of the fish should be presented to Mellitus as evidence that the tale was true. This is supposedly the origin of the annual tithe of salmon that was paid to the Abbey by Thames fishermen.

The quiet cloisters is said to be the phantom monk's favourite walk. (Peter Spiro–FOTOLIA)

There was definitely a small community of monks living on the island by the late eighth century. Offa's Charter, which dates from AD 785, speaks of, 'St Peter and the people of the Lord dwelling in Thornea at the terrible place known as Westminster', the word 'terrible' here referring to the place's religious connection and implying 'awe-inspiring'. In around AD 960 St Dunstan enlarged the monastery and a century later the Saxon king Edward the Confessor (reigned 1042-1066) built a large new church on the same site. According to legend, Edward had vowed to make a pilgrimage to Rome to give thanks for his success in subduing his kingdom but the English nobles opposed this plan, fearing for the king's safety if he left the country. As a compromise the pope sent Edward a message, telling the king he would be absolved from his vow on condition that he build or restore a monastery in honour of St Peter the Apostle. Before the bishops conveying the pope's message arrived, a hermit told the king that St Peter had appeared to him in a dream, foretelling the bishops' return and pointing out the old monastery on Thorney Island as the site for his new church. The new building was duly consecrated on 28 December 1065 but Edward was too ill to attend the ceremony and died a few days later, on 5 January 1066.

The death of another king – Henry IV (reigned 1399-1413) – supposedly fulfilled a prophecy here. Henry had been told he would die in Jerusalem, which he understood to mean he would be killed in the Crusades, but during a visit to Westminster Abbey in 1413 he collapsed in the Abbey's 'Jerusalem Chamber' and died the evening before he was due to depart for the Holy

Land. This tale, a variation on a popular legend, was dramatised by Shakespeare in *Henry IV Part 2* (Act 4, Scene 5): the king asks Warwick if the room in which he collapsed has any particular name, to which Warwick replies, 'Tis call'd Jerusalem, my noble lord.' To this, Henry exclaims:

> Laud be to God! Even there my life must end.
> It hath been prophesied to me many years,
> I should not die but in Jerusalem,
> Which vainly I suppos'd the Holy Land.
> But bear me to that chamber; there I'll lie:
> In that Jerusalem shall Harry die.

Of the various ghosts said to haunt Westminster Abbey, the best known is the phantom of a tall, thin monk referred to as 'Father Benedictus'. Sallow-skinned, with a domed head and a prominent hooked nose, his large brown eyes are penetrating and deep-set. The phantom appears to be quite solid and witnesses do not immediately realise they are looking at a ghost. Two young female friends saw him one Saturday afternoon in 1900 as they sat with their backs to the south transept, waiting for evensong to commence. One of the women felt someone staring at her and looked around, directly into the eyes of a Benedictine monk. She later reported that the monk, 'was standing with his hands hidden in the sleeves of his habit and his cowl half back from his head. He swept the assembly with a very contemptuous glance then looked straight at me again.' The monk slowly walked backwards, pausing every now and again to gaze with scorn upon the people in the transept, until after around twenty-five minutes he disappeared through the wall. He may have been seen again in April 1923, when three people saw a brown-robed figure inside the abbey.

The phantom monk's favourite walk is the quiet cloisters where he is said to appear often between 5 and 6 p.m. Walk may not be quite the right word though, for Father Benedictus stands an inch or so above the stone floor, perhaps because of the differences in floor level caused by wear and resettlement and centuries of alterations to the building. It was in the cloisters in 1932 that a spiritualist claimed to have successfully communicated with this ghost, which spoke to him in what sounded like 'Elizabethan' English. The cowled figure approached to within 5ft of where the spiritualist stood waiting with two companions and before vanishing told him that he had been killed during the reign of Henry VIII.

There are at least two stories about how Father Benedictus died. According to one version, he did indeed die during Henry VIII's reign, killed by robbers who were after treasure stored in the Chapel of the Pyx. The second story is similar but places his death during the historic robbery committed in 1303. At this time, the low vaulted Pyx Chamber was used by the king (Edward I) as a treasury and in 1303 thieves broke in and stole a fortune in money and plate. Unfortunately, although this fits in neatly with the tale of 'Father Benedictus', there does not seem to be any record of any monk being killed inside the Abbey either during this robbery or in the time of Henry VIII.

The robbery of 1303 features in another legend associated with Westminster Abbey. At the entrance to the octagonal Chapter House is a battered old oak door that stands some 6½ft tall. The top of the door was cut off at some time in the past and the original door is thought to have been over 9ft tall. In the nineteenth century someone noticed small fragments of hide adhering to this door and a legend developed that this was human skin, supposedly the skin of a punished man. The most popular version of this tale says that Richard de Podelicote (and perhaps his accomplices), having been found guilty of the theft from the Pyx Chamber, was

Statue of King Charles I in Trafalgar Square.

Banqueting House in Whitehall. Charles I was beheaded outside here in 1649.

hanged and flayed and his skin nailed to this door as a warning to other would-be thieves. Another tale claims that a man had been found guilty of sacrilege during the Middle Ages and, again, was flayed and his skin nailed to the door as a warning. However, in 2005 tests funded by English Heritage showed that the fragments of hide still adhering to the ancient wood are not human after all but cow hide, which would have covered both sides of the door and been painted over as decoration.

Peter Underwood (1973) wrote that a policeman on duty outside the abbey on an autumn night some years before had witnessed a man in ecclesiastical robes hurry towards the unlit building and melt straight through the closed western doors. As the shocked policeman approached the abbey to take a closer look he felt someone tap his shoulder and turned around to see an eerie procession of black-clad men walking in pairs with their heads bowed and their hands clasped before them. In silence, the men made their way towards the abbey and, like the first figure, they melted through the closed doors. Stepping up to the door, the policeman listened and heard 'sweet and plaintive' music coming from within the Abbey but he was momentarily distracted when someone walked past him and when he listened again there was only silence. The policeman was not the first to see a procession of ghostly figures at the Abbey. Another was the noted poet, painter and visionary mystic, William Blake. Between 1772 and 1779, the young Blake was apprenticed to an engraver named James Basire, who sent him to make drawings of the Abbey's sculptures and it was on one of these visits that Blake had an early vision. He saw a great procession of monks and priests, choristers and censer-bearers, moving through the aisles and galleries, and as he watched the Abbey filled with the majestic swell of organ music and the chant of plain-song and chorale.

Another ghost said to haunt Westminster Abbey is that of John Bradshaw, president of the High Court of Justice that ordered the execution of King Charles I in 1649. Bradshaw had trained as a lawyer and throughout the English Civil Wars was a staunch Parliamentarian, aiding Oliver Cromwell in the fight against the monarchy. Under Bradshaw's presidency, the King was tried in Westminster Hall for high treason and 'other high crimes against the realm of England' and on 27 January 1649 the sentence of death was pronounced. King Charles I was to be executed as a, 'tyrant, traitor, murderer and public enemy to the Commonwealth of England'. He was beheaded on the morning of Tuesday 30 January on a scaffold erected outside the Banqueting House at Whitehall. In March, Bradshaw was made president of the Council of State, the executive body of the Commonwealth, but he retired from politics in 1654, unhappy with changes wrought by Cromwell. Several months after Cromwell's death in September 1658, Bradshaw was again made a member of the Council of State and in June 1659 he became Commissioner of the Great Seal. He died later that year on 31 October 1659 and, like Cromwell before him, was buried in Westminster Abbey. Their bodies were not destined to remain there for long, however.

Bradshaw's ghost supposedly haunts the deanery. There are reports of his apparition being glimpsed here, although this haunting more often takes the form of heavy footsteps heard at night, both in the passage and on the stairs. His ghost is also said to haunt Red Lion Square in Holborn, approximately one-and-a-half miles north-northeast of the abbey. The square is on the site of the Red Lion Fields, close to where an old inn known as the Red Lion once stood, and Bradshaw's ghost appears here in the company of two other phantoms, those of Cromwell and Henry Ireton, Parliamentarian General and Cromwell's son-in-law. For their crime of regicide, the three men underwent a macabre punishment together in death. After King Charles II returned to claim his father's throne in 1660, those who had been directly responsible for his father's execution were brought to trial. Not even death provided refuge from this retribution

Above: *Red Lion Square, Holborn.*

Right: *Statue of Oliver Cromwell outside the Houses of Parliament.*

A soldier of the First World War. The phantom of a khaki-clad soldier from this period reputedly haunts the vicinity of the grave of the Unknown Warrior. (Duncan Walker, iStockphoto.com/duncan1890)

and Bradshaw, Cromwell and Ireton were posthumously attained for high treason. Their bodies were exhumed and it is believed that the coffins containing the corpses of Cromwell and Ireton were taken to the Red Lion Inn on 26 January 1661. Unlike the others, Bradshaw's body had not been embalmed and the stench was such that his corpse was not taken to join them for another few days. From there the three coffins were taken to (it is usually said) Tyburn. There, on 30 January – the anniversary of the king's execution – they were hanged until sunset, then cut down, decapitated and the bodies thrown into a pit beneath the gallows. The heads were fixed to spikes outside Westminster Hall. The three ghosts are said to walk across the square in a straight line, cutting across at a diagonal from south to north, oblivious to the present-day pathways. They stride together three abreast – some say arm-in-arm – and appear to be deep in conversation with one another, their heads apparently restored to them in spirit.

The most poignant of the abbey's ghosts is that of a First World War soldier said to haunt the area around the grave of the Unknown Warrior. Located at the western end of the nave, the grave is covered by a slab of black marble quarried in Belgium and is filled with soil from France. In 1920, the bodies of four (some say five or six) unknown British servicemen were exhumed from the battlefields of the Aisne, Arras, the Somme and Ypres and taken to the chapel at St Pol, where they were covered with Union Flags. There, Brigadier General L.J. Wyatt selected one of the bodies at random. The others were reburied but the selected body was brought to England where on 11 November it was buried with great and sombre ceremony. The inscription on the marble slab reads:

Beneath this stone rests the body of a British warrior, unknown by name or rank, brought from France to lie among the most illustrious of the land and buried here on Armistice Day, 11 Nov. 1920, in the presence of His Majesty, King George V, his ministers of state, the chiefs of his forces, and a vast concourse of the nation. Thus are commemorated the many multitudes who during the Great War of 1914-1918 gave the most that man can give, life itself, for God, for King and Country, for loved ones, home and Empire, for the sacred cause of Justice and the freedom of the world. They buried him among the kings because he had done good toward God and his house.

The phantom said to appear from time to time a few feet away from this grave is that of a khaki-clad soldier in the mud-stained uniform of a First World War infantryman. He wears no cap or helmet and his head is bowed in sadness. His eyes are filled with pleading and his arms are sometimes stretched out as if asking for help. He is a silent ghost although at least one witness felt that he was trying to say something. While most claim that it is the spirit of the Unknown Warrior himself, some say that it is the brother of the man who lies buried here, but whoever he is his true identity will remain a mystery.

Westminster Bridge

Westminster Bridge spans the Thames by the Houses of Parliament, linking Westminster with the area of the east bank now watched over by the London Eye. The current bridge is the second to stand here. The first opened in 1750, before which the only bridge crossing the river was London Bridge; however, it had a worrying tendency to sway on its foundations and was eventually replaced by the current structure, which opened in 1862.

A phantom boat supposedly surges through the Thames around here. It is crewed by two or three men who can be seen on deck although their faces are in shadow and their identities cannot be discerned. The boat is seen to approach the bridge and pass beneath one of the arches, but what happens from that moment on is a mystery for it never reappears on the other side.

Other tales from Westminster Bridge have a unifying dark undercurrent running through them, in that they all involve suicide. One such story was recorded by Elliott O'Donnell (1933). On a sunny summer's day a young man was travelling towards Westminster aboard one of the ferry steamboats that used to carry passengers between here and Greenwich. He could not help but notice a particular lady sitting somewhat apart from the other passengers for, although her face was concealed beneath a black veil, her figure, hands and general bearing suggested that she was young and attractive. The boat steamed its way through the water, and just moments before it passed beneath Westminster Bridge the lady suddenly stood up and leapt overboard into the river. After the briefest moment of initial shock, the young man jumped to his feet, pulled off his coat and dived in after her. He was an excellent swimmer but despite his best efforts he could find no trace of the lady and at last was forced to conclude that it was too late to save her, and that she had already sunk into the cold depths of the Thames. He swam back to the steamboat where the other passengers helped to pull him up out of the water and back on board. As he sat there, cold, miserable and shivering, the captain came up to him but instead of delivering the expected words of consolation told him, 'You are the third person this week who has jumped in after that creature.' The young man was utterly confused by this: did the captain mean she had been playing some kind of prank? But if that was the case, what had happened to her? Why had he not spotted her in the water? Solemnly, the captain answered his tumbling questions. 'What becomes of her is more than I or anyone else can tell you,' he stated, and revealed that at some

Left: *Westminster Bridge. (Stephen Finn – FOTOLIA)*

Below: *Evening draws in on Westminster Bridge. (davidmartyn – FOTOLIA)*

time in the past a young lady of identical appearance really had jumped from this steamboat at just that spot. She had drowned. Since then, her apparition had appeared on the boat from time to time, re-enacting the last desperate moments of an unknown but presumably tragic life.

Another suicide that haunts Westminster Bridge is a male figure who is said to throw himself over the side into the dark waters just as Big Ben sounds midnight. He has been described as having a pale face and a black moustache, and wearing a top hat and frock coat, and he is reputedly the ghost of a man who ended his life here at the stroke of midnight on 31 December 1888. The apparition is often said to materialise on this date, plunging into the water just as the New Year begins. Some claim that this is the ghost of Jack the Ripper. In this legend, Jack the Ripper was a medical man who was aware that the police suspected him and were closing in. Knowing it was only a matter of time before he was caught he cheated them by killing himself; this explains why the Ripper was never caught and why the Whitechapel murders ended when they did. (The savagely butchered remains of Mary Jane Kelly, generally believed to have been the Ripper's final victim, were discovered on 9 November 1888.) This story is perhaps rooted in the fate of Montague John Druitt, one of numerous men suspected of having been Jack the Ripper. Born in 1857, Druitt was a barrister, schoolmaster and keen cricketer. At around the beginning of December 1888 he was dismissed from his teaching position for unknown reasons and shortly afterwards committed suicide. His body, weighted down by stones in his pockets, was fished out of the Thames at Chiswick on 31 December that year, and it was estimated that it had been in the water for around one month. Some – but by no means all – Ripperologists take this as evidence of Druitt's guilt, pointing out that there were no further killings after his death. (For other ghost stories connected with the Ripper murders see 'The East: Ghosts of Jack the Ripper's Victims', p. 115).

Slightly less grim is the tale recounted to O'Donnell by a policeman and recorded in *More Haunted Houses of London* (1920). One morning, at about 2 a.m., the policeman was crossing Westminster Bridge with his back to the Houses of Parliament when he heard the sound of footsteps running after him. He turned around to find a well-dressed and very beautiful woman standing before him. She pleaded with him to accompany her at once for someone she had just left was in 'great trouble', and she was so earnest in her appeals that the policeman, although he was due to report in to his sergeant, agreed to help. She led him back the way he had come and then off the bridge, onto the Victoria Embankment where he saw a woman obviously just about to throw herself into the river's murky brown waters. He reached the woman an instant before she jumped and after a short struggle managed to pull her back from the edge to safety. It was only then that the startled policeman realised that this woman was identical in every respect to the one he had met on the bridge. He looked around for the first woman but there was no sign of her and so, reasoning that the two women must be twins or at least close relatives, he asked the second woman where she had gone. She was baffled, replying that she had no relatives at all. In fact, she had not a friend in the world. Moreover, she had been completely alone on the Embankment and could offer no explanation as to the identity of her mysteriously vanished double. (For a similar tale set on another bridge, see 'Waterloo Bridge', p.65).

Another policeman was crossing the bridge late one night on his way home to Kennington when he felt someone tap him on the shoulder and clearly heard a woman's voice say, 'This is the spot, this is the spot'. According to *Elliott O'Donnell's Casebook of Ghosts* (edited by Harry Ludham, 1969) the policeman turned around to ask what she meant and was surprised to find that there was nobody anywhere near him. Puzzled, he shrugged the incident off and continued on his way, but the same thing happened to him on the next two nights, on both occasions in the same place and at about the same time. The following night he was again walking across the bridge and was approaching the spot where he fully expected the mystifying experience to occur for a fourth time. Instead, a man suddenly rushed across the pavement just in front of him and began to climb over the side, obviously intent on throwing himself into the river. The policeman rushed over and pulled him back before he could leap. There was no struggle; the man seemed resigned that he should live for at least a little longer and quietly gave his story. He had, he said, been a clerk until losing his job, since when he had been unemployed and desperate for work. Finally, he decided that enough was enough; he could take no more and now wanted only to end the pain of struggle. Taking pity on the wretch, the policeman judged that he was not about to repeat his suicide attempt that night and rather than take him to the station he handed over what few pennies he could afford on condition that the ex-clerk promised to persevere in his search for a job the following morning. The man agreed and there they parted company. The policeman never heard from him again and could not say what had become of the poor fellow, but although he had crossed Westminster Bridge countless times since he had never again felt the ghostly tap on his shoulder and the mysterious warning voice.

CHAPTER FOUR

THE RIVER THAMES: AROUND THE VICTORIA EMBANKMENT

Cleopatra's Needle

'The bleak wind of March made her tremble and shiver; but not the dark arch, or the black flowing river.' In Thomas Hood's poignant poem about a woman's suicide, *The Bridge of Sighs* (1844), the river is the Thames, and the dark arch refers to Waterloo Bridge. This bridge and the riverfront along the nearby stretch of the Victoria Embankment have long held an unenviable reputation, being said to exert an almost hypnotic pull on the fatally depressed.

This area is also the haunt of one of London's most startling ghosts, a naked figure that might initially be mistaken for another suicide. It supposedly appears in the vicinity of Cleopatra's Needle, that enormous obelisk of red granite hewn from an Egyptian quarry thousands of years ago. The obelisk stands around 69ft high, weighs approximately 180 tons and juts from the Embankment a short distance south of Waterloo Bridge. Despite its name, it has no direct connection with the illustrious Egyptian queen, dating from around 1450 BC, centuries before her reign. It bears hieroglyphic inscriptions to Thothmes III and Ramses II, and originally stood at Heliopolis in Egypt before being moved to Alexandria in 12 BC, after which it lay prostrate on the Alexandrian sands for centuries. In AD 1819 it was presented to 'The British Nation' by Mehemet Ali, Viceroy of Egypt, in commemoration of the actions of Lord Nelson at the Battle of the Nile in 1798 and Sir Ralph Abercromby at the Battle of Alexandria in 1801 during the wars against Napoleon Bonaparte. But the obelisk remained in Egypt until 1877 when Erasmus Wilson FRS finally funded its transportation. In that year, the monolith was encased in a great iron cylinder named the *Cleopatra*, which acted as a floating pontoon to be tugged to England by the steamship *Olga*. It was a perilous voyage and disaster struck on 14 October 1877 when the *Cleopatra* capsized in a storm in the Bay of Biscay. Six men lost their lives in the efforts to rescue the *Cleopatra*'s crew, but the cylinder itself remained afloat. It was eventually retrieved and brought to England and the obelisk was at last erected on the Victoria Embankment in 1878. In the autumn of 1917, it had another narrow escape when a German bomb exploded nearby, the shrapnel damaging one of the two bronze male sphinxes standing guard at its base. But despite its age and the dangers it has weathered, the ancient obelisk endures, declaring in the words of Alfred, Lord Tennyson, 'I have seen the four great empires disappear. I was when London was not. I am here.'

Little is known of the ghost, or possibly ghosts, that haunt the vicinity of Cleopatra's Needle. Passers-by have been disturbed by strange sounds at night: some have reported hearing mocking

Above: *The Victoria Embankment, seen from Golden Jubilee Bridge.*

Left: *Cleopatra's Needle.*

Opposite: *Sphinx standing guard at the base of Cleopatra's Needle.*

laughter or else the sounds of someone groaning in misery. Others have been startled by the aforementioned sight of a tall naked man abruptly running out from the shadows. This shocking apparition climbs over the parapet and throws himself over the wall into the 'black flowing river' below, but then there is only silence. No one ever hears the splash of him hitting the water and no body is ever discovered. What may be a second phantom around Cleopatra's Needle was described by author Steve Jones (1986) as a hazy and troubled figure. The figure is seen standing on the wall, apparently deliberating whether or not to take the final fatal step. If he is approached he jumps, but he disappears before he reaches the river's surface and once again no sound is heard.

Waterloo Bridge

Waterloo Bridge has its own ghost stories, one of which was recounted to Elliott O'Donnell some time prior to 1920 by a tramp who had spent many a night sleeping rough around here. The tramp had been leaning over the side of the bridge one night, staring into the dark waters below and contemplating ending his life when his brooding was interrupted by a drunken young man reeling past. The youth was dressed in the height of fashion and the tempting glint of gold from a watch and chain on his waistcoat was enough for the tramp to temporarily abandon any thought of suicide. Stealthily, he set off after the youth who before long stumbled to a halt and leaned against the bridge parapet for support. The tramp crept up behind him, nearer and nearer until he was just a few inches away then, with the young man still oblivious to his predicament,

Waterloo Bridge.

reached out as quietly as possible, opened his fingers and grabbed for the watch – only for his hand to pass through empty air and hit the parapet. The young man had vanished. Badly shaken, the tramp hurried away from Waterloo Bridge, no longer considering suicide and anxious only for the company of living human beings.

There were also once stories of a headless ghost haunting the bridge. These followed a gruesome discovery in 1857. At about 5.30 in the morning of Friday 9 October two lightermen named James Barber and Frank Kelsby were rowing out to a barge when they spotted a carpetbag on one of the bridge's abutments. They took the bag onto their boat and when they later opened it in the presence of their employer they were horrified to find it contained the dismembered remains of a human body. Much of the flesh had been removed from the bones and when the police surgeon pieced together what was left he found that the skeleton's head, hands and feet were missing. Who the victim was and exactly how he came to be stabbed seven times in the chest and twice in the abdomen have never been resolved although various theories have been put forward over the years. At the time, a popular idea was that the murdered man was a foreign sailor, possibly from one of the several Swedish ships anchored in the Thames at the time. A different theory was held by Sir Robert Anderson, who came to believe that the victim was 'an Italian Police agent who had been sent to London on a special mission'. Sir Robert, who was appointed assistant commissioner of Scotland Yard's Criminal Investigation Department at the beginning of investigations into the Jack the Ripper murders in 1888, published his memoirs, *The Lighter Side of My Official Life*, in 1910. In them, he stated his belief in the claim that the

Stories of a headless ghost followed a gruesome discovery on one of Waterloo Bridge's abutments in 1857.

agent had been working undercover to infiltrate a group of Italian revolutionists in Soho and was murdered by them after they discovered his identity. They sawed his corpse into pieces and tried to get rid of the remains by burning them but this proved too time-consuming so they disposed of the rest of the body in the river.

If Sir Robert was correct, it would not be the only time Waterloo Bridge has become embroiled in a shadowy underworld of secret agents and killings. More than a century later the bridge was the setting for one of the strangest murders in London's history. In September 1978, a Bulgarian dissident named Georgi Markov was waiting at a bus stop on the bridge when a man jabbed him in the leg with the tip of his umbrella. Three days later, Markov was dead, and it was later established that he had been injected with a small pellet containing the poison ricin. The assassin who wielded the specially adapted umbrella/weapon is claimed to have been an agent of the Bulgarian secret services.

A final ghostly tale from Waterloo Bridge is set during the 1940s and is strikingly similar to a tale told earlier of Westminster Bridge a little further south (see 'Westminster Bridge', p. 59). It relates the experience of a police officer who was crossing the bridge one foggy night when a well-dressed but hysterical young woman rushed up and frantically begged him to follow her. Someone was about to jump into the river, she sobbed, and they must hurry to prevent the tragedy. Together, they hastened off the bridge and along the Embankment towards Cleopatra's Needle, arriving just in time to catch hold of a young woman as she prepared to throw herself into the waters. As the policeman pulled the would-be suicide back to safety, he was astounded to see that she was identical to the young woman who had fetched him from the bridge. He looked around to where the first woman had been standing scant moments before but now there was nobody to be seen. There was only the ancient obelisk looming over the dark riverside.

The Theatre Royal, Drury Lane

Perhaps it has to do with the powerful emotions conjured onstage and evoked within the rapt audience, or with the atmospheric surroundings of a grand old building, or even with the deliberate confusion of the here and now with other places and distant times. Or perhaps it has something to do with the superstitious nature of many of the people who work in theatres. Whatever the reason, there seems to be a rule that theatres should be haunted, and of all theatrical ghosts the best known is undoubtedly the silent phantom that stalks the Theatre Royal, Drury Lane: the Man in Grey. Although it is included in this section Drury Lane actually lies a short distance north of the Victoria Embankment, but it would be criminal to let geographic exactitude prevent this mention of one of London's most famous haunted buildings.

The Man in Grey
The story of the Man in Grey was already generations old by 1945 when theatre historian W.J. Macqueen Pope recorded it in his book, *Theatre Royal, Drury Lane*. Countless witnesses have claimed sight of this spectre and described him in similar terms. He is a young man of just over medium height, with a strong, handsome face, attired in clothing of the early eighteenth century. He wears, or sometimes carries, a tricorn hat and his hair is either powdered or covered beneath a powdered wig. Presumably he is a horseman, for he wears riding boots and a long grey riding cloak, beneath which a sword can be seen hanging from his waist. Unlike many ghosts he invariably appears during the day, between around 9 a.m. and 6 p.m., startling both cleaners and matinee audiences as well as actors and other theatre staff and visitors. He usually seems solid and perfectly clear so long as the witness does not approach too closely, in which case the apparition goes out of focus and vanishes. He has been seen sitting in a seat in the upper circle's fourth row but more often walking calmly along the back of the upper circle from one side of the auditorium to the opposite wall where he vanishes.

One sighting was in 1938. Shortly after 10 a.m., as actors rehearsed on the stage below, a cleaner walked into the upper circle and spotted someone sitting in the end seat on the centre gangway of the fourth row. The figure was clad in grey and wore an old-fashioned hat, which, coupled with the way he was watching the rehearsals, led her to assume he was one of the actors. Nevertheless, the cleaner felt she should make sure he was supposed to be there and so she set down her bucket and broom and went to speak to him. As she approached, he seemed to vanish and then reappear at the exit door on the right hand side of the circle, through which he then passed. Although she had never before heard of the Man in Grey, the description she later gave theatre staff matched perfectly that given by previous witnesses.

Macqueen Pope himself, in his aforementioned book, put it on record that he had, 'seen this apparition on numerous occasions', adding that he, 'has excellent sight, is not troubled mentally, has not a fantastic mind, and is not a Spiritualistic medium.' He was also present when writer James Wentworth Day saw what was probably the same ghost. The two men were among a group of six investigating the empty theatre following a spate of sightings; the others present included psychic investigator Harry Price and renowned stage magician Jasper Maskelyne. Wentworth Day was sitting in the seat where the previously mentioned cleaner had seen the apparition

Above: *The Theatre Royal, Drury Lane.*

Right: *The Man in Grey, Drury Lane's most famous ghost. (Anthony Wallis www.ant-wallis-illustration.co.uk)*

earlier that same year when the lady beside him suddenly gripped his arm and gestured towards a wall, whispering, 'Do you see that?' He looked to where she was pointing and saw an eerie glow following the Man in Grey's usual path around the back of the circle. He described it afterwards as a, 'grey pearly light, impalpable, hovering, [that] moved across the dark void of the central box. It moved with the odd uneven action of a man with a limp. [...] It was in mid-air – four feet above the floor. It moved unevenly. It was almost a shape, certainly no reflection.'

The many sightings of this ghost have passed into theatre legend. At one matinee performance in the 1930s, a lady in the upper circle asked a puzzled attendant if actors came into the audience during this play because she had seen a man wearing a hat, white wig and long grey cloak walk through the door just ahead of her. During the Second World War, the theatre was taken over by ENSA, the Entertainment National Service Association, and one autumn evening in 1942 their Broadcasting Officer Stephen Williams clearly saw the Man in Grey from the grand staircase. Another ENSA staff member knew nothing of the famed phantom until she spotted him in 1943. In September 1950, an actor was playing in a Saturday matinee performance of *Carousel* when his attention was drawn towards one of the boxes. When he first looked the box was empty, but the second time he glanced in that direction he saw a man standing there, swaying slightly. The man wore a grey cloak over a ruffled, long-sleeved shirt and as the figure raised one arm the actor realised he could see through the arm to the door behind it. It is even said that, at rehearsals for one play many years ago, the ghost was simultaneously seen by seventy of the hundred or so cast members on stage.

A Spiritualist once claimed the ghost was of a man named Arnold Woodruffe, but nobody really knows the identity of the Man in Grey. Not that this has prevented a legend developing to account for the haunting. The story goes that a wealthy young gallant came up from the country one day during the reign of Queen Anne (1702-1714) to see the London sights. Visiting the playhouse this young buck went backstage to meet the actresses, one of whom fell for his charms. Unfortunately for him, the girl's spurned lover was provoked into a fit of jealous rage; there was a fight, the young man was killed and his corpse quietly bricked up in the theatre. This suggestion was inspired by a gruesome discovery made in around 1848 during structural alterations to the theatre. Workmen noticed that a part of the main wall on the Russell Street side of the upper circle sounded hollow and asked their foreman for advice. The foreman spoke to his master who in turn consulted management and it was eventually decided that they should break through to find out what the problem was. Behind the wall they discovered a small chamber that had been bricked up long ago, and a man's skeleton. Among the old bones were a few scraps of cloth, which crumbled as soon as they were touched, but the workmen's attention was focused more on the dagger that protruded from the skeleton's ribcage. The skeleton had evidently lain in its hiding place for some considerable time for the wall had been left untouched during earlier rebuilding work in 1796 and after a fire in 1809. The Cromwellian design of the dagger hinted at a murder in the mid-seventeenth century, but the weapon might have been a theatrical prop. An inquest was held but in the absence of any real evidence an open verdict was returned and the bones were interred in a graveyard at the corner of Russell Street and Drury Lane, now a small open space called Drury Lane Gardens. Interestingly, the place where the skeleton was found corresponds with the part of the wall where Wentworth Day first saw the strange glow in 1938.

The Man in Grey is considered something of a mascot for Drury Lane, which is why the theatre has turned down at least one offer of exorcism. A long-standing tradition holds that this ghost's appearance during rehearsals or early performances heralds a successful run for that production.

Drury Lane Gardens; does the Man in Grey lie buried here?

Dan Leno

Another ghost said to haunt this theatre is that of the comedian Dan Leno. Born George Galvin in 1860, the son of a show-business family, Leno found early fame as a clog dancer and went on to become one of the greatest music hall performers of all time, starring in Drury Lane's Christmas pantomime every year from 1888 until his death in 1904. Several actors and stagehands have claimed encounters with his ghost here, in particular another popular comedian, Stanley Lupino, who described his experience at a charity luncheon in 1923.

Late one night after appearing in pantomime, Lupino found himself too tired to face the journey home and lay down to rest on his dressing-room couch. As he lay in the dim room he suddenly felt he was not alone. There was a sound like the soft swish of a curtain being drawn and he sat up just in time to glimpse a shadowy figure move across the room and out through a door without seeming to open it. A little groggy, he felt puzzled rather than afraid and sought out the theatre caretaker to ask if he had seen anyone. The caretaker told him that the two of them were quite alone in the building. Lupino returned to his dressing room and again lay down to rest but after a short while he heard another sound, this time very close to him. He sat up, catching sight of himself in the make-up mirror and was shocked to see a second face reflected next to his own. It was a deathly white but there could be no doubt that it was the face of Dan Leno. Terrified, Lupino fled the theatre to find somewhere else to stay the night. Only later did he discover that the room had been Dan Leno's favoured dressing room and the last one he had used.

Dan Leno's grave in Lambeth Cemetery.

Perhaps Lupino later grew accustomed to the haunted dressing room because according to Macqueen Pope he often claimed that Leno's ghost would visit him there to offer counsel and advice. Other performers have reported hearing a rhythmic drumming noise coming from the same room, supposedly the sound of Leno rehearsing his old clog-dancing routine. Stanley Lupino died in 1942 and now lies buried in South London's Lambeth Cemetery, united in death with Dan Leno whose own grave lies just a few feet to the left.

The Helping Hands

One of London's oddest ghost stories comes from the stage here, which is reputedly haunted by a pair of invisible helping hands. During the exceptionally long run of *Oklahoma!* following the Second World War there were numerous cast changes and at one point a young and relatively inexperienced actress named Betty Jo Jones came over from America to play the part of Ado Annie. This is a comedy role but the first few times she played here she did not receive the laughs she knew the part deserved. One night, as she was on stage with two other actors, Jones sensed the soft pressure of two hands on her shoulders gently guiding her towards a different position downstage. There she felt her body being eased into a new angle and received a reassuring pat on her back. She looked around but neither of the other actors was near enough to have

Stanley Lupino's grave in Lambeth Cemetery.

been responsible. The new position proved to be better for her role because now the audience responded much more positively to the comedy, laughing at all the right moments. The unseen hands continued to guide her throughout the rest of the performance and for the following three nights, and afterwards she continued to play the part as she had been shown, always with great success.

Another young actress, Doreen Duke, also benefited from this kindly phantom when she auditioned for a role in *The King and I*. She desperately wanted to perform at Drury Lane and so was extremely nervous as she waited to be called to the stage. Then she felt a pair of hands rest calmly upon her shoulders and was enveloped by a warm feeling of helpful guidance. The hands stayed with her when her name was called and they guided her to a particular position on-stage. Reassured by their presence, she sang her piece and afterwards was rewarded with a friendly pat on the back. She got the part. The hands continued to guide and comfort her throughout the rehearsals and up to and including the show's successful opening night. Then with one final pat they left her, although she continued to sense a comforting presence every now and then.

Some believe this mysterious phantom to be another manifestation of the theatre-loving Man in Grey. Others, however, feel that the presence's kindly nature and skill at evoking laughter point to this being another ghost – that of history's greatest clown, Joseph Grimaldi.

Left: *Grimaldi's ghostly face is said to watch the performers on stage. (Anthony Wallis: www.ant-wallis-illustration.co.uk)*

Below: *The Joseph Grimaldi Park.*

Joseph Grimaldi's grave.

Joseph Grimaldi

The son of an Italian actor also named Joseph, Grimaldi was born on 18 December 1778. By the age of three he had already made his stage debut. He would go on to find lasting fame as the 'father' of today's circus clowns, using his athletic prowess and genius for comic timing to make early nineteenth century audiences roar with laughter. The character he created – a white-faced combination of simple-minded innocent and cunning rogue – would be adopted by generation after generation of clowns after him, and clowns are still known as Joeys today in his memory. It is said that at one of his shows in July 1807, a deaf and dumb man sitting in the audience found his act so hilarious that his power of speech returned and he cried out, 'What a damned funny fellow!' Sadly, Grimaldi's extremely physical performances took their toll on his body. His final public performance was at Drury Lane on the night of 28 June 1828, by which time he could no longer stand and had to be carried on-stage in a chair in which he remained for the entire performance. Despite this, the ailing clown could still make his audience laugh and it was a triumphant exit.

Grimaldi died on 31 May 1837 at No. 33 Southampton Street (now Calshot Street) and was buried nearby in St James's churchyard on Pentonville Road, a short walk east from King's Cross railway station. The churchyard was later deconsecrated and part of it, including Grimaldi's tomb, survives today as the Joseph Grimaldi Park. His ghostly face, eerily painted in white clown make-up is said to appear behind people sitting in one of the Theatre Royal's boxes, gazing over their shoulders and watching the performers on stage. (His apparition is also said to haunt London's Sadler's Wells Theatre, where a very similar story is told.)

A trio of Charleses

Drury Lane boasts not one, nor two, but three separate phantoms named Charles! Charles Macklin was born in Ireland as Charles McLaughlin at the end of the seventeenth century. A distinguished actor and playwright, he is also remembered for his violent nature and uncontrollable temper, which once resulted in the death of a fellow actor in Drury Lane's Green Room. On 10 May 1735, an argument broke out between Macklin and Thomas Hallam over who had the right to wear a particular wig. During the heated exchange, Macklin thrust at Hallam with his walking stick, the stick piercing Hallam's eye. The stricken man fell to the ground and later died as a result of the injury. Although Macklin was prosecuted over this affair he was never sentenced and he went on to live an extremely long life, not dying until 1797. At the time of his death, he claimed to be 107 years old, although there is some doubt over the truth of this. A grim phantom, tall and emaciated with an unattractive, heavily lined face has been identified as Macklin's ghost, and this supposedly stalks in front of what used to be the pit, appearing most often in the early evening shortly before the start of a performance.

The second ghostly Charles is Charles II, the king who gave the theatre its royal charter. A man spotted this phantom one summer afternoon in 1948 as *Oklahoma!* was playing on stage. According to this witness, the ghosts of Charles II and a crowd of courtiers walked down the side gangway of the stalls, climbed onto the stage and disappeared among the unsuspecting actors.

The third Charles was seen during the Boer War period (1880-1801 and 1899-1902), when a lady from Birkenhead attended a matinee performance with her brother and her sister. This was before the auditorium was reconstructed in 1921-1922 and they were sitting in three gangway seats in the front row of the dress circle, on the left-hand side of the house. Nobody else was sitting in their row and because the other end of the row was flush with the wall anyone wishing to enter would have had to walk past them. Yet during the interval the lady glanced across and was surprised to see a man sitting in the same row, a few seats away. She pointed him out to her sister because he was bizarrely dressed in out-dated clothing and wore unfashionably long hair. The two ladies chatted about him for a few moments until their brother asked what they were talking about. When they told him, he looked across but saw only empty seats. The play restarted and the three of them returned their attention to the stage although the ladies occasionally looked over to see the man still sitting there. At some point, however, they noticed that he had gone, despite there being no way he could have left without passing them. The first lady wrote to Macqueen Pope to tell him of their experience, but when she first contacted him there was no way to identify the man from her description. Then in 1945 she wrote to him again after seeing a photograph in his book *Theatre Royal, Drury Lane*; the photograph was of actor-manager Charles Kean who had died in 1868 and the lady was absolutely certain that it showed the very same man she and her sister had seen sitting in the theatre that afternoon years before.

The entertainer Ivor Novello once wrote that, 'Drury Lane is not just a theatre – it is a tradition, a national treasure and should be included in the "musts" for every visitor to London.' And when you do visit this city you could do worse than heed Macqueen Pope's advice for he suggested coming to Drury Lane *twice*: once to watch the show and then a second time to look out for the theatre's many ghosts.

CHAPTER FIVE

THE CITY: LONDON'S HEART

The Bank of England

The Bank of England is often referred to as 'The Old Lady of Threadneedle Street', a nickname that can be dated back to a 1797 political cartoon depicting the Bank as an elderly woman protesting at the advances of Prime Minister William Pitt the Younger. But some people prefer to believe that the original Old Lady is the female phantom long claimed to haunt this building at the hub of the United Kingdom's financial system.

Founded in 1694, the Bank was originally located in Mercers' Hall in Cheapside and then in Grocers' Hall in Princes Street, before it moved to Threadneedle Street in 1734. For the next hundred years it expanded as it gradually acquired the surrounding land and premises. The solidly forbidding, fortress-like structure visible today occupies about three acres in the City's main financial district. First set up to act as the Government's banker and debt-manager, the Bank's role has evolved over the years and it is now the United Kingdom's central bank. Nationalised in 1946 following the Second World War, the Bank became independent in May 1997 when the Government gave it responsibility for setting short-term interest rates.

This is the site of one of London's lost traditions: the special military detachment known as the Picquet (pronounced Picket) which, apart from a few brief periods, dutifully guarded the Bank each night for almost two centuries. The tradition began in 1780 to protect the Bank after it was attacked by a mob during the Gordon Riots but was ended in 1973. These days, the Bank relies more on hi-tech – if less colourful – security measures, yet even these seem incapable of keeping out the ghosts said to walk here.

The Gordon Riots showed that the Bank was vulnerable to attack from the west, from the roof of the neighbouring church of St Christopher-le-Stocks, and so legislation was passed in the 1780s to deconsecrate and pull down that building. With the church gone, the Bank expanded its premises and the old churchyard later became a garden area within the Bank. This Garden Court is reportedly haunted by the sad ghost of a woman named Sarah Whitehead. Sarah was the sister of Philip Whitehead, a clerk at the Bank who in 1811 was found guilty of forging an acceptance to a bill and was sentenced to death. Philip's friends kept news of his crime and execution from Sarah in a misguided attempt to protect her, until one day, puzzled by her brother's long absence, Sarah visited the Bank and asked after him. When the young employee to whom she spoke innocently revealed the truth, the terrible shock unhinged Sarah's mind and,

The Bank of England.

unable to accept the pain, she refused to admit that her brother was no more. Thereafter, every day for the next quarter of a century, no matter what the weather, Sarah Whitehead returned to the Bank looking for the brother she believed still worked there.

The sight of her forlorn figure lingering by the entrance was unmistakeable, draped from head to foot in black mourning clothes, her cheeks crudely and incongruously rouged beneath a black veil. From time to time, she would wander inside to ask a member of staff if her brother was available, to be politely told that he had not been in yet that day. Sadly, she would ask the clerk to tell Philip she had called for him before returning to keep her lonely vigil at the door. The Bank clerks felt much compassion for her and it is said that they cared for her as much as they could, often giving her money as they passed by and even providing a room for her.

A less romantic version of the story tells of a different motive for Sarah's vigil, saying that she believed the Bank had defrauded her of a vast sum of money. One day, Sarah confronted Baron Rothschild on the steps of the Stock Exchange and demanded payment, whereupon the Baron calmly handed her a half-crown on account, promising that the rest would follow. Sarah smiled, thanked him and cheerfully went on her way.

Sarah died at the age of around sixty and was buried within the Bank's environs, in the old churchyard of St Christopher-le-Stocks. She kept up her daily ritual until the last, and even death does not seem to have put an end to her ceaseless search as she is supposed to return here in spirit form. The story of this ghost dates back to around 1840 and as mentioned above has been suggested as the origin of the expression 'Old Lady of Threadneedle Street'. This cannot

The Bank of England is known as 'The Old Lady of Threadneedle Street'.

be the case, however, because this nickname for the Bank already existed some years before. The phantom has also become known as The Black Nun, the name used by the Bank employees of her day on account of her attire. The phantom is sometimes said to linger at the Bank's entrance as Sarah continues her endless quest and there are also tales of her spirit roaming the building's corridors, stopping passers-by and asking if they have seen her brother, but most stories agree that her ghost haunts the small enclosed garden hidden away deep within the building and it is here that many people claim to have caught a glimpse of the spectre.

One person who reported seeing this apparition was R. Thurston Hopkins, a man with an abiding interest in ghost stories whose account was reproduced in Jack Hallam's *Ghosts of London* (1975). Hopkins was in the gallery looking down onto the garden when a friend suddenly pointed out the figure of a woman wearing a black dress moving uncertainly along a path made up of old gravestone slabs. 'It's the Black Nun!' gasped his friend. Hopkins described how the woman wandered along with a hesitant, uncertain air, almost as if she were blind and trying to feel her way. Abruptly, she dropped to her knees and began to beat her hands desperately against one of the slabs, sobbing and moaning in uncontrollable grief. The apparition was visible for no more than a few moments but Hopkins was left in no doubt that he had seen the fabled Black Nun ghost.

Another ghost story is told of a gigantic figure, said to be 8ft tall, that wanders the Bank's corridors and in years gone by occasionally unnerved the soldiers of the Bank Picquet by shaking their rifles. The story of this sizeable spectre has its roots in real life, although the height of the gentleman involved appears to have become somewhat exaggerated over the years.

William Daniel Jenkins was an exceptionally large man for his time, standing 6ft 7½in tall. He worked as a clerk here during the eighteenth century, dying at the age of thirty-one on 24 March 1798. During his last days he had become increasingly fearful that 'resurrectionists' (body snatchers) would steal his corpse to sell to a surgeon for study and so, after his death, his friends sought and received permission to have his body buried in the safety of the Bank, in the Garden Court that had once been a churchyard. Jenkins's enormous lead coffin, measuring 7½ft in length, was rediscovered in August 1933 during building work and, in accordance with a 1923 Act of Parliament governing the treatment of this former churchyard, his remains were removed to Nunhead Cemetery.

It would seem that neither of the Bank's ghosts has been sighted in recent years and although somebody might occasionally report a cold draught or an odd noise within the building, these are not necessarily due to any paranormal cause. As Bank spokesperson Vanessa Crowe commented when I contacted her in July 2006, 'Much of this can be explained by the air conditioning and the movement of the building; although it is strongly constructed – a steel skeleton on which the stone is hung – it does move.'

A fascinating insight into the history of the Bank of England is available by visiting the Bank's museum. Admission is free and it is open to the public from Monday to Friday, apart from Public and Bank Holidays.

St Paul's Cathedral

The famous dome of St Paul's Cathedral has dominated London's skyline for centuries. Here is the very heart of this great city, where the now buried Walbrook River flows in a valley between the ancient hills of Cornhill to the east and Ludgate Hill to the west. The cathedral stands atop the latter and tradition holds that it was built on the site of a Roman temple dedicated to the goddess Diana. Legend also has it that below the cathedral, within Ludgate Hill, is buried the head of King Lud, after whom London itself was named. (It is uncertain whether King Lud ever really existed though, as he may have been an invention of the twelfth-century Welsh writer and chronicler, Geoffrey of Monmouth.)

The first Christian cathedral to occupy this site was dedicated to St Paul in AD 604. After its destruction by fire, it was rebuilt between 675 and 685, but this new building fell to Viking raiders in 962. Once again, St Paul's was rebuilt and once again it was destroyed, burning to the ground in 1087. A legend states that although this fire destroyed practically everything else it miraculously left untouched the resting place of St Erconwald (or Erkenwald), the Bishop of London, who had been interred here following his death around 693. Construction of a new cathedral began in the late eleventh century and the body of King Henry VI (reigned 1422-1461, and 1470-1471) later lay in state here after his mysterious death in the Tower of London (see 'The Tower of London: The Wakefield Tower', p. 99). This pious and scholarly king had been imprisoned during the Wars of the Roses and rumours swiftly spread that his death was the result of murder. As his corpse lay in St Paul's, it reportedly began to bleed and as it was believed at the time that the body of a murdered man would bleed in the presence of his killers, this was taken as proof that the king had not died a natural death.

During the Reformation in the sixteenth century, the cathedral fell into disrepair and further damage was suffered in 1561 when a lightning strike destroyed the spire and started another blaze. Sir Christopher Wren was asked to repair St Paul's during the 1660s but before work could begin flames yet again consumed the cathedral (as well as much of the rest of London) in the Great Fire

Right: *St Paul's Cathedral, seen from Ludgate Hill.*

Below: *St Paul's Cathedral.*

These battered sixteenth-century statues housed within the vestry porch of St Dunstan-in-the-West church in Fleet Street are thought to represent King Lud and his two sons.

of 1666. Wren's plans for a new St Paul's were approved in 1675 and construction lasted between that year and 1710. The completed building actually differs significantly from the agreed plans and draws greatly upon an earlier design of 1673 which had not been approved, but few would argue that the cathedral we see today is anything short of magnificent. Wren himself now lies entombed in the crypt, in such noble company as Lord Nelson and the Duke of Wellington.

The best-known ghost story from St Paul's comes not from the crypt, as might be supposed, but from the Chapel of All Souls, located at the cathedral's west end, on the ground floor of the north-west tower. Also known as the Kitchener Memorial Chapel, this was in 1925 dedicated to the memory of Field Marshal Lord Kitchener and to the servicemen killed during the First World War. The apparition that allegedly haunts this area of the cathedral is of an elderly clergyman who wears the clerical dress of a long-gone age. Sometimes the ghostly strains of a high-pitched, whistled melody are also heard drifting through the cathedral. It is said that the apparition vanishes after a short time, fading away into the wall at a specific place, and that one day as structural repairs were being carried out in the chapel workmen discovered a small concealed door in the stonework at that same spot. When the door was opened, a narrow staircase was revealed, winding upwards through the massive walls towards a hidden passage, the existence and purpose of which had long been forgotten.

Another ghostly tale dates from 1899. One summer's day in that year, an American lady and gentleman visiting the cathedral were walking down the central aisle when they were both

The north-west tower of St Paul's Cathedral; the Chapel of All Souls is situated on the ground floor of this tower.

badly frightened by a 'great black cloud' that suddenly rose up from the ground before them and ascended into the air about 20ft before suddenly vanishing. They stated that the cloud had been unlike anything they had ever seen before and that it gave the impression of being alive. This tale was recorded in O'Donnell's *Ghosts of London*, which also mentions that another lady, while enjoying a peaceful break in the cathedral one day, noticed a woman kneeling in one of the aisles ahead of her, seemingly searching the ground for something. Thinking she might need some assistance, the lady stood up and started to approach the kneeling woman, when she felt someone touch her on the shoulder. She turned around at once but there was no one there, and when she looked back the woman too had vanished. When the exact same thing happened to her again a few days later, at about the same hour as before, the poor lady was overcome with an 'eerie feeling' and hurried out of the cathedral as quickly as she could.

St Paul's Cathedral is usually open to sightseers from Monday to Saturday and is an important heritage site. Primarily, however, it remains a place of worship; indeed, as the capital city's cathedral, St Paul's is in a very real sense the spiritual centre of this nation.

The Old Bailey

Peer through the iron gates barring the entrance to Amen Court in Warwick Lane and you will see a quiet enclave of old houses overshadowed by an ancient wall of crumbling brown bricks. For many years, stories have circulated about something malign and sinister haunting this wall, a

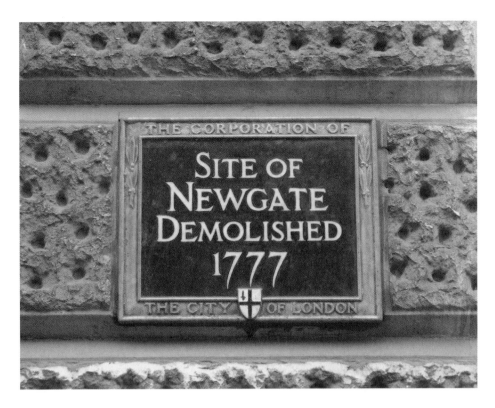

Above: *Plaque on the wall of the Old Bailey in Newgate Street.*

Right: *The statue of Justice without the usual blindfold stands atop the Old Bailey.*

Opposite above: *There are stories about something sinister haunting the old wall at the back of Amen Court.*

Opposite below: *The Central Criminal Court, popularly known as the Old Bailey.*

black and shapeless mass that slithers across the top of the old bricks in the dead of night. Some tales speak of a scraping noise accompanying the dark form – perhaps the scuffing of heavy boots against the stone, and of the rattle of unseen chains. These stories are probably related to a certain building that once stood nearby, for this is an area of London that has known a great deal of suffering and death.

Behind the wall is the Central Criminal Court, more commonly known as the Old Bailey and it stands on the site of London's most infamous prison. This was Newgate, whose 'dreadful walls', wrote Charles Dickens in *Oliver Twist*, had 'hidden so much misery and such unspeakable anguish'. On the other side of this wall was the route along which prisoners were once marched on the way to and from their trials, their footsteps clanging on the iron grating that covered the floor. The grating gave this place the name 'Birdcage Walk', but it had another name, too – 'Dead Man's Walk' – for the flagstones visible beneath this grating concealed graves where many executed prisoners lay buried in quicklime.

In Roman days, this was the site of one of the main gateways into the city of London. A prison was first constructed here in the late twelfth century and was rebuilt several times over the centuries until being demolished in the 1770s. The new prison that replaced it was itself badly damaged after being set on fire during the Gordon Riots of 1780. Rebuilding was completed in 1782 and the following year London's gallows were moved to Newgate from Tyburn. For much of the next century, prisoners' executions were carried out publicly in the open area in front of Newgate Prison, where they attracted enormous crowds of spectators. This lasted until 1868, when executions were taken out of the public eye and moved within the prison walls, where death sentences continued to be carried out until the beginning of the twentieth century. Newgate Prison's 'dreadful walls' were finally pulled down in 1902 when it and the court next door were demolished, and work began on the Old Bailey, which opened in 1907.

The Black Dog of Newgate

Some speculate that the black shape haunting the wall at the back of Amen Court is a supernatural residue of the wickedness of Newgate's gaolers, accumulated over the centuries. More probably, the story has its roots in a sixteenth-century poem titled *The Black Dog of Newgate*, although perhaps this poem was itself inspired by pre-existing tales of a terrible black phantom seen here. The poem was written in around 1596 by Luke Hutton while he was a prisoner here and the quotes that appear below come from a 1638 version of the tale titled *The discovery of a London Monster, called, the Blacke Dogg of Newgate*. Hutton himself was later released from Newgate but failed to mend his ways and was soon afterwards sentenced to death for robbery, dying on the gallows in York in 1598.

The phantom of the poem's title was, 'a walking spirit in the likenesse of a blacke Dog, gliding up and down the streets a little before the time of Execution, and in the night whilst the Sessions continued'. Its origins were described as dating back to the days of King Henry III (reigned 1216-1272), during a period in which London was struck by a severe famine. Faced with starvation, the incarcerated inhabitants of Newgate turned to cannibalism as their only means of survival. Most at risk were prisoners who had already grown too weak to offer much resistance and also those poor unsuspecting wretches who found themselves newly cast into this 'Denne of misery'. Desperate for sustenance, the starving inmates seized one of these new arrivals, a scholar imprisoned upon suspicion of conjuring and witchcraft, and killed and ate him. They deemed their victim to be 'passing good meate' but before long came to regret their actions because they began to see, or imagine that they saw, the scholar return 'in the shape of a black Dog walking up and downe the Prison, ready with his ravening Jawes to teare out their bowels'.

Wealthy people could watch executions in comfort from the Magpie & Stump public house opposite Newgate Prison (the pub has since been rebuilt).

Night after night, the trapped inmates fancied they caught sight of the beast and heard 'strange groanes and cries' as if fellow prisoners were being ripped apart by those hellish jaws and devoured. Their terror increased and 'such a nightly feare grew amongst them, that it turned to a Frenzie, and from a Frenzie to Desperation' until at last in panic they killed their guard and escaped. But no matter how far they fled from the prison's dungeons, there was no escape from the terrible knowledge of their crime of cannibalism and 'whither soever they came or went they imagined a Blacke Dog to follow'.

Jack Sheppard

Others believe that the black shape is the ghost of Jack Sheppard, re-enacting the notorious robber's final and most renowned jailbreak. Among the people holding this view was a clergyman from St Paul's Cathedral who in 1948 claimed to have seen the dark apparition on the wall on several different occasions.

Jack Sheppard was born in Spitalfields, in London's East End in 1702. As a young man he was apprenticed to a carpenter but after a short time turned instead to crime and in 1724 was captured and imprisoned in the St Giles Roundhouse. He swiftly escaped from here and was soon robbing Londoners again. A couple of weeks later he was arrested for pickpocketing and imprisoned at Clerkenwell but once again he quickly escaped. Two months later he was recaptured by the thief-taker Jonathan Wild. Sentenced to death, Sheppard was taken to Newgate

Left: *Jack Sheppard was buried in the churchyard of St Martin's-in-the-Fields (near what is now Trafalgar Square).*

Opposite above: *Smithfield Market.*

Opposite below: *Peaceful West Smithfield Garden, just south of the market.*

and held in the condemned hold, yet again he managed to break out. Prisoners were permitted to speak with their friends through a hatch barred with large iron spikes, and Sheppard cut through one of these enough to enable him to snap it off and squeeze through the tiny gap. He did not remain free for long. A few days later, he was captured after robbing a watchmaker's shop in Fleet Street and was returned to Newgate. By now, Sheppard's multiple escapes from gaol had made him a sensation and Londoners flocked to Newgate to see the superstar criminal. Determined to prevent him absconding, the prison guards placed Sheppard in a strong-room known as the 'Castle', where he was chained securely to the floor with his hands cuffed and his legs fastened with irons.

Now Sheppard staged the most amazing of all his escapes. Working his hands out of the cuffs, he used a small nail to open the padlock securing his chains to the metal staple in the floor. Still encumbered by the fetters on his legs he began to climb up the chimney but found his path blocked by an iron bar set into the brickwork. With a piece of the broken chain he picked out the mortar around this bar until he could break it free, then climbed further up the chimney until he emerged into an long-unused room above the 'Castle'. Here he found a large nail, used it to wrench off the lock securing that room's door, and eased himself into a passage. Forcing open more locked and bolted doors, Sheppard finally found his way outside and onto the prison roof. But he was too high above the ground to risk leaping down and so he was forced to retrace his journey all the way back to the 'Castle' to retrieve his blanket before returning to the roof, spiking the blanket to the stone wall and silently sliding down to freedom.

Unfortunately for Sheppard he was recaptured two weeks later and once again sent back to Newgate, this time staying until his final journey to the gallows at Tyburn where he was

executed in November 1724. His body was buried the same evening in the churchyard of St Martin's-in-the-Fields.

Tales from Inside the Prison

Although the massive walls of Newgate Prison have now been torn down, stories of ghosts within them are still remembered. On a number of occasions, prison officers heard footsteps echoing through the gloomy stone corridors, steps that had a curious unevenness to their rhythm as if the walker had a limp. Usually, when the officers investigated to see who was there, the steps would stop and on only one occasion was the culprit seen. In December 1891, an officer was working late in the vicinity of Dead Man's Walk when he heard footsteps coming from the direction of that passage. As he listened, they grew louder, seeming to approach, and his first thought was that it must be the chief warder doing his rounds. He quickly realised however that this stealthy and uneven sound was not the familiar measured tread of the chief warder and so he opened the grille in his office door to peer out into the passage. As the grille opened it revealed a horrific face pressed against the other side, a face with the corpse-white skin and green bruised throat of a hanged man. Then the face vanished. The officer opened the door and found the passage deserted, and later learned that the last man to have been buried under Dead Man's Walk had been lame.

Thurston Hopkins once told Peter Underwood about a strange happening in the prison chapel, located deep inside Newgate. One night a chaplain was alone in the quiet, dimly lit chapel when the black curtains of the condemned pew were suddenly pulled open to reveal the figure of a man with a gaunt, 'skull-like' face sitting there. Some weeks later, the chaplain happened to see a portrait of a forger named Henry Fauntleroy who had been executed at Newgate in 1824. It was unmistakably the likeness of the apparition he had seen that night.

Hopkins wrote down another of Newgate's ghost stories in his book, *Ghosts Over England*, stating that he had been told the tale by Mr Scott, the Chief Warder. It involved Mrs Amelia Dyer, known as 'the Reading baby-farmer'. She had been paid to look after unwanted babies but instead drowned them in the Thames and continued to draw money for their keep. For this evil crime, Dyer was sentenced to death and was sent to Newgate to await execution. As a prisoner, Scott recalled, Dyer was well behaved but 'she was too submissive and oily for words. [Her] eyes were always watching me, and her hands folded on her black dress … Those glittering eyes of hers instilled into me a strange feeling of disquiet and foreboding'. On 10 June 1896, as Dyer was being taken to the execution shed, she paused and looked directly at Scott, telling him, 'I'll meet you again some day, sir.'

One night a few years later, a short time before Newgate was finally closed, several of the warders were sitting in the Keeper's room, sharing a bottle of whisky to celebrate their final week of duty. A glass window in the door to this room looked out onto the Women Felons' Yard. Suddenly, Scott felt a strong sensation of being stared at and remembered Dyer's voice saying that she would meet him again some day. He looked towards the door and saw staring back at him through the glass the dark-eyed, thin-lipped face of Amelia Dyer. The apparition gave what Hopkins described as a 'sad enigmatical look' and then was gone as if she had walked on past. Scott leapt to his feet and pulled open the door only to find the yard empty save for a woman's handkerchief lying on the wet flagstones.

Another tale has it that when Scott was once photographed outside the execution shed, the developed photograph showed behind his shoulder a face that should not have been there. The features were those of Amelia Dyer.

The hauntings within Newgate Prison seem to have continued until the very end of that hated institution. Elliott O'Donnell once interviewed a prison official and his wife who had

Above left: *Memorial to Sir William Wallace on the wall of St Bartholomew's Hospital.*

Above right: *Martyrs' memorial on the wall of St Bartholomew's Hospital.*

been sitting in their kitchen the night before work began to demolish the prison. Just after they finished their supper, the bell in the condemned cell began to ring. 'The bell was in the corridor,' the official remembered, 'and could only be rung by someone within the cell pulling the lever, and as we knew we were alone in the building we were not a little surprised and startled.' Nervously, they went to investigate but found nobody there, just an empty room in a dying building, and the old bell still violently swinging to and fro.

Today, a black-cloaked apparition is said to haunt the site of Newgate Prison, appearing inside the Old Bailey in response to miscarriages of justice. It is believed to be the ghost of someone wrongly accused of being a highwayman, who was hanged and buried here for crimes of which he was wholly innocent.

Smithfield Market

In 1174 a clerk named William Fitzstephen described, 'a smooth field where every Friday there is a celebrated rendezvous of fine horses to be sold, and in another quarter are placed vendibles of the peasant, swine with their deep flanks, and cows and oxen of immense bulk.' That area has become known as Smithfield (the name probably comes from 'smooth field'), famous for its meat market, which is one of the largest of its kind in the world. As well as hosting the market, this area, which was once an open space lying just outside the city walls, was used for public events such as jousting and tournaments – and executions.

Hundreds were put to death here over the centuries, among them Sir William Wallace ('Braveheart'), the Scottish patriot who fought to free his country from English rule. Condemned as a traitor, he was hanged, disembowelled, beheaded and quartered, and a granite plaque on the wall of St Bartholomew's Hospital marks the approximate spot of his execution on 23 August 1305. It would not be surprising for such a hideous death to give rise to ghost stories, but the ghosts that haunt Smithfield are said to come from a later era, from the terrible religious persecutions of the Tudor queen who earned the name 'Bloody Mary'.

Mary I (reigned 1553-1558) was the daughter of King Henry VIII, who had split England from the Roman Catholic Church. During the reign of her half-brother, Edward VI (1547-1553), the Protestant religion had become established in England but when Edward died and Mary became queen she set about restoring Catholicism to her country. On her command, Protestants were ruthlessly persecuted as heretics and it has been estimated that around 300 were burned to death at the stake, many of them at Smithfield where they were made to face east towards the church of St Bartholomew the Great. The exact site of the burnings was discovered in the mid-nineteenth century during excavations for a sewer, when charred human bones were found 3ft below the surface of the ground. There is now a memorial to the Protestant martyrs close to this site, on the wall of St Bartholomew's Hospital.

Mary supposedly decreed that green wood should not be used for the pyres in case the smoke suffocated the heretics, killing them before they suffered the agony of burning to death. People walking through this area alone late at night or early in the morning have apparently heard ghostly moans and the harrowing screams of Mary's victims, as well as the crackling of blazing wood and, from to time, the sickening stench of burning flesh.

CHAPTER SIX

THE TOWER: TOWER HILL AND THE TOWER OF LONDON

Tower Hill

The *Mabinogion*, a collection of stories from medieval Welsh manuscripts, tells of the giant Bran. Believed to have originated as an ancient – possibly pre-Celtic – god, Bran is in this later tradition described as the king of Britain who invades Ireland at the head of the Hosts of the Island of the Mighty. While his followers sail across the sea, Bran simply wades across, and in Ireland he lays himself over the River Shannon as a bridge for his men to walk over. The inevitable battle is hard-fought because the Irish make use of a magical cauldron (an earlier gift to them from Bran) that has the power to reanimate the dead: eventually only seven of the Host remain alive. Bran himself is mortally wounded by a poisoned spear and he orders his surviving followers to cut off his head and carry it back to Britain. Their mystical homeward journey, during which Bran's head remains able to converse with them, takes decades but when they at last return they bury the head beneath London's 'White Hill', facing towards France. So long as Bran's head remained buried there, it was said, no invader could cross the sea to attack Britain. (According to the Welsh *Triads*, King Arthur later removed this talisman, declaring that he alone should be Britain's guardian. Another tradition holds that the mythical Trojan leader Brutus, founder of Troynovant – New Troy or London – was buried under this same hill.)

The 'White Hill' in Bran's story is believed to be Tower Hill and it was here that William the Conqueror later built the keep at the centre of what we today call the Tower of London. This keep became known as the White Tower, a name that may derive from the whitewashing of the exterior in the thirteenth century although some believe that the origin may be much older and lie with the 'White Hill'. Folklorist Jennifer Westwood has noted that the word 'white' in Welsh can mean 'holy' and so William possibly selected this site for his keep in part because of the powerful associations it already held.

'Bran', meanwhile, may translate as 'crow' or 'raven', and just as Bran's head is supposed to keep invaders at bay, legend asserts that the presence of ravens within the Tower of London protects the realm. Indeed, should the ravens ever leave then the Tower will supposedly crumble and disaster befall Britain, a prophecy that almost came to pass during the Blitz in the Second World War when at one stage only a single raven remained living there. The ravens' presence at the Tower has long been protected but nobody knows for certain when the tradition began. It may have begun as late as the nineteenth century although legend claims that the birds have been here much longer,

Should the ravens ever leave, the Tower of London will supposedly crumble and disaster befall Britain.

This small memorial in Trinity Square Gardens marks where the execution scaffold once stood.

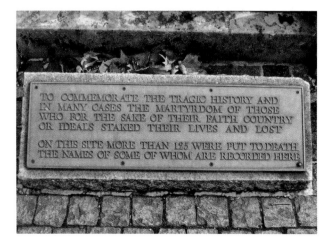

The plaque on the execution site in Trinity Square Gardens.

strutting around the grounds and croaking from the mighty stone walls for long centuries. The story goes that in the seventeenth century John Flamsteed, 'astronomical observator' to King Charles II, asked for the ravens to be removed because they were interfering with his work observing the heavens from the central keep's northeast turret. The king ordered them destroyed but when he was warned that without the ravens the Tower and then his kingdom would fall, he changed his mind and decreed that at least six ravens should always remain within the castle walls.

Ravens traditionally have an affinity with places of death and execution and so it is little surprise to find them associated with this area of London. Centuries of bloody history have been played out within and around the confines of the Tower of London, and of course many ghostly tales have arisen. The ghosts appear even before you enter that grim fortress, which we shall come to in a moment. There is a popular misconception that all of the Tower's prisoners were put to death privately within the castle itself but in fact all but a few of the executions were carried out outside the Tower, a little further up Tower Hill. In this public venue many thousands of spectators would throng to watch, the unruly mob crowding onto viewing stands erected around the execution scaffold, eager for a good view of the grisly proceedings. Today, the site where the execution scaffold stood is marked by a small memorial on the ground in Trinity Square Gardens, a short distance north of and overlooking the Tower. Here a plaque reads, 'To commemorate the tragic history and in many cases the martyrdom of those who for the sake of their faith, country or ideals staked their lives and lost'. Approximately 125 prisoners were put to death here, mostly by beheading, which was seen as an honourable death befitting those nobles and gentlemen found guilty of treason. Common criminals met their end here too, despatched by hanging, and heretics were burned in great bonfires.

One night, a sentry on patrol at the castle entrance saw a group of figures slowly making their way down Tower Hill towards him. This is said to have happened during the Second World War (or according to some accounts the First World War), but the uniforms worn by these figures struck the sentry as distinctly old-fashioned. The group carried a stretcher and on this, the sentry then saw, lay a decapitated corpse, the head tucked in between one arm and the torso. Nearer and nearer the figures came – and then they vanished. When the sentry's detailed report of the incident was investigated it was realised that his description of the old-fashioned uniforms matched those that had been worn in the Middle Ages by the Sheriff's Men. The other details fitted too: a prisoner about to be executed would have been taken from the Tower of London and handed over to the Sheriff to be escorted up Tower Hill to the execution site. Afterwards, the Sheriff's Men would carry the corpse back down to the Tower for burial, and it was seemingly one such scene that the sentry had seen re-enacted, hundreds of years after the event.

The Tower of London

When the Tower of London was built, bulls' blood was supposedly mixed with the mortar as a symbol of strength and lasting power. Perhaps this is why the fortress has endured for almost a thousand years. The first structure was the great keep now known as the White Tower, but the building and rebuilding continued over the centuries as the fortress grew in an almost organic fashion and almost every tower, home and stretch of wall here has acquired its own uncanny tales. There are so many in fact that it is possible to mention only a handful here; for further information, see particularly two excellent books by Geoffrey Abbott (details in bibliography), both available from the Tower's gift shops. For anybody interested in London's ghost stories, a trip to the Tower is a must.

The Byward Tower.

The Byward Tower

Beyond the visitor entrance, the first tower you pass through is the Middle Tower gatehouse and from here a causeway leads from over the now-dry moat to another gatehouse, known as the Byward Tower. In her *Haunted Royal Homes*, Joan Forman records how a Yeoman Warder (one of those Tower residents and guardians fondly known as Beefeaters) told her of a colleague's strange experience here. While on duty, this gentleman looked up from his work to see a group of four or five Yeoman Warders seated around a log fire smoking long pipes. Disturbingly, the room in which the men were sitting looked unfamiliar and this, coupled with their uniforms which dated from an earlier period, gave the impression of an event that had happened many years before. The unnerved witness hurried out of the room and when he returned a short while later, the men had gone and all once again looked as it should.

Another Yeoman Warder was on night watch at the Byward Tower on a bitingly cold winter's night in February 1983. Sitting in the guardroom at around 2.30 a.m. he glanced up towards the door and was shocked to see someone looking back towards him. Although the figure vanished after a few seconds, the face had unmistakably been that of Sir Walter Raleigh. That famous Elizabethan gentleman had spent many years imprisoned in the Tower of London, and his apparition looked much as he appears in the portrait of him that hangs in his study in the Bloody Tower. About one-and-a-half years later a different Yeoman Warder saw the same apparition in the same place.

St Thomas's Tower and (on the right) Traitors' Gate.

St Thomas's Tower and Traitors' Gate

Running east from the Byward Tower, parallel to the river, is the section of the Outer Ward known as Water Lane. The gloomy water entrance opposite the Bloody Tower is known as Traitors' Gate because so many accused of treason were brought here by boat from their trial at Westminster, passing through this gate on their way to imprisonment and, often, eventual death. Before this entrance was built, the Bloody Tower itself stood on the river's edge. It was the construction of the newer gate and the adjoining St Thomas's Tower that gave rise to what is probably the Tower of London's oldest ghost story. This tells that the king, Henry III, was concerned that the new gate weakened the fortress's southern defences and so he had a tower built above it. The taxes raised to cover the cost of this construction were the cause of much resentment amongst Londoners. In 1240, during the building work, a storm arose, the tower's foundations gave way and the tower collapsed into a pile of rubble. The king ordered work to begin again but exactly one year later the tower collapsed again. A superstitious tale swiftly spread to explain the destruction: apparently, a priest had seen the ghost of St Thomas à Becket standing on the tower, striking off stones with his cross and proclaiming that the defences were not for the benefit of the kingdom but, 'for the injury and prejudice of the Londoners, my brethren'. Only too aware that it had been his own grandfather (Henry II), whose hasty words had resulted in the murder of 'that turbulent priest', the king arranged for the new tower to be named in honour of the murdered archbishop and for an oratory dedicated to him to be built within.

The water entrance known as Traitors' Gate.

St Thomas's Tower has acquired other ghostly tales, too. Before it was opened to the public it provided accommodation for Tower officials and their families and also, apparently, a phantom monk who has been seen walking from room to room clad in a brown habit. In 1974, a family living here heard the 'slap slap' sound of the monk's sandaled feet walking across a wooden floor, evidently an echo from the past because their rooms were at that time fully carpeted. An earlier resident, Major General Sir George Younghusband, KCMG, KCIE, CB, the then Keeper of the Jewel House, was also reportedly troubled by strange happenings. On several occasions he saw the door to one room slowly open, remain still for a few seconds and then softly close itself. Other people have heard the sobbing of a young child, who is never seen. A further tale tells of a brigadier and his wife who were returning to their quarters in St Thomas's Tower after a walk when a Yeoman Warder asked whether they had visitors in their room. When they replied that they had not, the Yeoman Warder said that he thought he had seen a face looking down at him from one of the tower's windows but the brigadier's wife was unsurprised. 'Oh,' she answered calmly, 'is it there again?'

In December 1994, a Californian student was visiting England as part of a school group studying Tudor history. Standing at the foot of St Thomas's Tower she took a photograph of Traitors' Gate, and was astonished later to see a mysterious hand in the picture. It appeared to belong to someone standing just behind her, reaching over her right shoulder towards the gate, but she was sure nobody had been there. Moreover, the hand looked as if it belonged to someone from an earlier period. Possibly gloved and seemingly surrounded by a glowing halo, the lacy cuff at the end of the darker coloured sleeved suggested a Tudor or Stuart style cuff. Geoffrey Abbott, who discusses the photograph in his *Mysteries of the Tower of London*, sought expert opinion and was able to determine that the hand was not the product of a double exposure, nor had it been superimposed by any computer fakery. Traitors' Gate was also the area where, at around 7.30 a.m. on 11 March 1980, a passer-by spotted a flickering blue light beneath the archway. He looked across to see a group of men and women in Tudor clothing passing through the gate and into the Tower, moving slowly as if in a barge. His detailed description of the number of figures and their appearance suggested that he had seen a re-enactment of the moments in February 1542 when Queen Catherine Howard was brought here by boat to be incarcerated in the Tower, later to be beheaded on Tower Green.

The Wakefield Tower

A covered bridge connects St Thomas's Tower to the mighty Wakefield Tower. Traditionally this was once the prison of King Henry VI. A gentle and scholarly man, Henry was ill-suited to reign during the turbulent Wars of the Roses as the two branches of the royal house of Plantagenet – the House of Lancaster and the House of York – fought their bloody struggle for the English throne. In 1471, Henry was taken prisoner and incarcerated within the Tower of London. He would never leave alive, reputedly being murdered in the small oratory in the upper chamber of the Wakefield Tower. On the night of 21 May 1471, whilst kneeling at prayer, Henry was, 'stikked with a dagger, full of deadly holes'. The assassin is said to have been Richard, Duke of Gloucester, later the infamous King Richard III (reigned 1483-1485), possibly acting on the orders of the new Yorkist king, Edward IV (reigned 1461-1483). Henry's wan apparition is said to appear in the vicinity of the chapel between 11 p.m. and midnight, the hour at which he was so brutally slain. However, it is now believed unlikely that Henry VI was really imprisoned in the Wakefield Tower. By 1471, this tower had become a storehouse for official documents and it is more probable that he was actually held a short distance further along Water Lane, in the Lanthorn Tower.

The Lanthorn Tower

A spiral staircase leads up out of the Wakefield Tower and onto a high battlemented wall that connects to the Lanthorn Tower. This wall forms part of the fortress's inner wall. Running parallel to it, on the right, is the outer wall and below, between the two walls, is the stretch of Water Lane where a sentry came under a mysterious attack at about 8.30 p.m. on 19 October 1978. It was a dark and moonless night although the area was well illuminated by security lights. As the sentry paced his route, he felt small stones rattle against his boots. Puzzled but not unduly concerned, he continued patrolling and another stone hit his boot, then another and then another. Calling out to another sentry, they agreed to swap patrols and now the second sentry began to be pelted with small stones. There was no wind that could have blown stone flakes from the wall and they could only conclude that someone unseen was throwing them. The two men called out the guard and the area was searched, but nobody was found.

Odd happenings have also taken place within the lower part of the Lanthorn Tower, which the Custody Guards were using as their control point during their nightly patrols early in 1976. One guard saw another pass by a frosted glass window and assumed that his colleague was visiting the washroom at the end of that corridor. He was mystified later to learn that the man had never left his chair all that evening. That guard had his own strange experience a short while later. They had left to patrol different buildings and when he returned to the Lanthorn Tower he thought

The Wakefield Tower.

he could hear his colleague moving around nearby, having apparently returned before him. In fact, his colleague was still out on patrol. In 1980, something took to interfering with the electric switches in this office. Despite ensuring their kettle was switched off when not in use, guards returning to it would find that the switch had been flicked back on. The refrigerator, on the other hand, would often be discovered switched off.

The Bloody Tower gateway

The forbidding Bloody Tower gateway leads through into the Inner Ward. In his 1950 book *His Majesty's Tower of London*, Resident Governor and Major of the Tower, Colonel E.H. Carkeet-James, OBE, MC, told how one night between the two world wars an officer of the Brigade of Guards was returning to his quarters after attending a dance. At this arch he was overcome by a 'most queer and utterly distasteful atmosphere' and felt a desperate need to escape. The next thing he knew, he was standing about 300 yards away on the steps of the officers' mess, sweating and out of breath. He had evidently sprinted there although he had no memory of it. Carkeet-James stressed that the officer had been completely sober at the time, as well as in the peak of health, being then in training with the British Olympic Games team.

The Bloody Tower

The gateway leads to the entrance to the Bloody Tower. This was constructed in the early 1220s, with its upper parts largely rebuilt in the second half of the fourteenth century. By the mid-sixteenth century it had acquired the macabre name by which it is now famous: 'Bloody', for this is traditionally where the young 'Princes in the Tower' were imprisoned and murdered.

The Lanthorn Tower.

Upon the death of King Edward IV in April 1483, the throne passed to his twelve-year-old son who became Edward V but the boy king would never be crowned. His uncle Richard, Duke of Gloucester, was given the role of protector to Edward and his younger brother Richard, Duke of York, and from that moment he effectively became England's new ruler. In June, the deceased Edward IV's marriage to Elizabeth Woodville was declared to have been invalid, a ruling that bastardised the two boys and meant that neither could legally succeed their father. This left their uncle Richard next in line of succession and later that month he acceded to the throne as King Richard III. Under their uncle's protection the boys were kept, it is said, in the upper chamber of the Bloody Tower where they could be seen through the windows or upon the battlements, happily playing together. Then one day they vanished from sight, never to be seen again, and a rumour spread that they had been murdered. Many blamed Richard III for their supposed killing although there is no conclusive evidence for this. In 1674, the bones of two children were discovered beneath an outer stairway of the White Tower and, although their identity has never been confirmed, they were reburied in Westminster Abbey as the remains of the two princes.

Current thinking is that the princes were probably held in the White Tower rather than the Bloody Tower, but it is in and around the latter that their silent, pitiful ghosts are held to appear. A 1901 book by Ronald Sutherland Gower entitled *The Tower of London* tells that the 'two small ghosts, hand in hand, clad in white nightgowns' were sighted here in the nineteenth century. A later witness was the daughter of a Yeoman Warder whose family lived in the Bloody Tower during the First World War. Her bedroom was the room in which the princes were supposedly killed and one day she climbed up the winding staircase to her room, opened the door and was startled to see 'two boys in funny clothes' on her bed. She cried out to her parents who came

Above left: *The Bloody Tower.*

Above right: *Ralegh's Walk.*

running up but when they arrived they found the room empty, with only a very noticeable chill in the air to indicate that anything strange had occurred.

The lower chamber is known as Ralegh's Study after Sir Walter Raleigh, an unwilling occupant of the Bloody Tower for many years. ('Ralegh' is an alternative spelling of the more common 'Raleigh'.) The room is furnished much as it might have appeared during the adventurer's incarceration here. A favourite of Queen Elizabeth I (reigned 1558-1603), Raleigh fared less well under her successor James I (reigned 1603-1625) and in 1603 he was sentenced to death on a trumped-up charge of plotting against the king. Receiving a last-minute reprieve he was instead imprisoned inside these cold and damp stone walls where, during his lengthy stay, he wrote his *The History of the World*. In 1616, he was released on condition that he led a gold-seeking expedition to the Orinoco basin, but a clash there with the Spaniards provoked an international incident. Keen to pacify the Spanish, the king invoked the suspended sentence and on 29 October 1618, Raleigh was beheaded at Old Palace Yard at Westminster. His phantom has been seen silently floating through the rooms of the Bloody Tower and also upon the stretch of battlemented wall adjoining this tower – known as Ralegh's Walk – where he often strolled during his years here.

The Queen's House
West of the Bloody Tower, on the southwest corner of Tower Green, stands the black-and-white timber-framed building that was originally known as the Lieutenant's Lodgings. Since the reign

of Queen Victoria this has been named for the reigning monarch; it is presently known as the Queen's House and was previously the King's House. Not open to the public, this fine Tudor building is home to the Resident Governor of the Tower, and Carkeet-James records how in 1947 an eminent peer of the realm who believed himself to be psychic visited this building and assured the occupant that 'there are no evil spirits in this house. It is a happy house. There may well have been unhappy spirits here in the past but they have departed now.' Despite his confidence, the Queen's House retains its reputation for being haunted.

One spectre here is known as the Grey Lady and it is said that only women will ever see her. Another is the apparition of a man in medieval dress that was seen in an upper corridor during the 1970s. Visitors have complained of penetrating chills in certain rooms, and of inexplicable noises including footsteps and religious chanting. There are stories of pitiful groans being heard and of the noise of instruments of torture being applied, echoes perhaps of times when prisoners were brought here for interrogation.

Particularly important prisoners were sometimes confined either in this building or in the Bell Tower behind it, which can only be accessed from here. One such resident was Queen Elizabeth I (when she was still Princess Elizabeth), and it may have been her phantom that was encountered one evening in April 1994 by a secretary working here on her own. As she climbed the stairs to fetch some papers from an upper room she found herself confronted with a woman standing motionless before her. Time seemed suspended as she stared in shock at the apparition, which she was later able to describe as having a white collar and red hair. She also noted the interesting detail that the apparition seemed to exist only 'from the waist up, as if in a portrait'.

Another eminent prisoner confined here was Elizabeth's mother, Anne Boleyn, the second wife of King Henry VIII. Desperate for a male heir and in love with Anne, Henry was eager to rid himself of his first wife, the ageing Catherine of Aragon, but the Roman Catholic Church refused to grant him a divorce. The King's solution was to split from Rome and create a new Church with himself at its head. He and Anne married in secret in early 1533 and Henry later had Thomas Cranmer, the Archbishop of Canterbury, declare his first marriage null and void. In September, Anne gave birth to Elizabeth but her marriage to Henry deteriorated and he began courting other women. The birth of a son might have saved her but after a miscarriage in 1534 and delivery of a stillborn son in 1536, Henry had her sent to the Tower charged with multiple adultery, including incest with her brother. Although the charges were almost certainly false, Anne was found guilty and sentenced to death. An eerie atmosphere supposedly permeates the room next to that in which Anne passed her last few days of life and people have caught the lingering aroma of perfume hanging in the air here. To some visitors, the room feels menacing and there is a story that children who have slept in this room have awoken in terror, feeling themselves being slowly suffocated. Anne Boleyn was beheaded on 19 May 1536, on Tower Green.

Tower Green

Tower Green is the neatly trimmed grassy area outside the Queen's House. Something thought to be Anne Boleyn's ghost has been seen drifting across this grass, from the Queen's House towards the scaffold site in front of the Chapel Royal of St Peter ad Vincula. Although most executions were carried out publicly outside the Tower walls (see 'Tower Hill', p. 93), seven prisoners were executed privately on scaffolds erected on this spot: William, Lord Hastings in 1483; Anne Boleyn in 1536; Margaret Pole, Countess of Salisbury in 1541; Catherine Howard and her lady-in-waiting Jane, Viscountess Rochford, in 1542; Lady Jane Grey in 1554; and Robert Devereux, Earl of Essex in 1601. In 2006 a new sculpture – a glass pillow, indented as if an invisible head rests upon it – was placed on the spot to commemorate their deaths.

The Queen's House.

In 1972, a nine-year-old girl was visiting the Tower with her parents for the first time. Standing by the scaffold site, the family was listening to a guide recite the names of those killed here and when he mentioned Anne Boleyn the girl whispered to her mother, 'They didn't chop her head off with an axe. They did it with a sword.' Apparently, she had 'seen' the execution and was able to describe the event in detail. Her comment was correct because, unusually, Anne was beheaded not with an axe but with a sword, by an executioner brought in from Calais especially for the task.

The most gruesome death on this site must be that of the elderly Margaret Pole, Countess of Salisbury, executed here in 1541 aged around seventy. After Henry VIII's break with the Church of Rome, the Countess remained faithful to Catholicism. The King tolerated her but was enraged when her son Reginald, Cardinal Pole, sent Henry a copy of his treatise denouncing the monarch's actions. Unable to act directly against the Cardinal in Italy, Henry took out his fury on the Pole family. One of the Countess's sons (Henry, Lord Montagu) was executed on Tower Hill in January 1539 for plotting against the State and in March of that year the Countess herself was sent to the Tower. It was widely expected that the harmless old woman would eventually be released but on 27 May 1541 Henry had her executed, seemingly as revenge against Cardinal Pole.

There is doubt over the precise details of the execution but it is clear that it was a particularly barbaric affair. The popular version of events tells how the Countess refused to lay her head down meekly on the block, saying, 'So should traitors do, and I am none'. Instead, she twisted

The scaffold site on Tower Green.

in all directions, challenging the executioner that if he wanted to take her head he would have to cut it off as best he could. And so the executioner was forced to chase her around the block, hacking away at her neck with his axe until the screaming Countess finally succumbed to her wounds and he was able to decapitate her. The grisly scene is supposedly replayed each year on the anniversary of the Countess's horrific death.

Perhaps the most tragic ghost is that of the beautiful Lady Jane Grey, England's unwilling 'Nine Days' Queen'. Jane was the granddaughter of Mary Rose, Henry VIII's youngest sister, and when King Edward VI died in 1553 Jane found herself in the line of succession to the throne. The natural heir was actually Mary Tudor, Henry VIII's daughter by Catherine of Aragon, but Mary was a Roman Catholic whereas Jane was a strict Protestant, which made her politically more attractive to many powerful figures. In addition, the ambitious John Dudley, Duke of Northumberland, had already married his son Guildford to Jane, and Dudley persuaded the dying Edward to name Jane as his heir. And so, although she fainted when the idea was first put to her, the fifteen-year-old Jane reluctantly allowed herself to be proclaimed Queen. She reigned (in name only) for nine days but the English people rose up in support of Mary whom they knew to be their rightful monarch. Jane and her husband were arrested and confined in the Tower, and Mary was crowned Queen. On 12 February 1554, Jane watched from the window of her room in the Yeoman Gaoler's Quarters as her young husband was taken away to be executed on Tower Hill, and later she watched as his remains were returned to the tower for burial. That afternoon, Jane herself was beheaded on Tower Green. According to Carkeet-James, Lady Jane

Above: *The Chapel Royal of St Peter ad Vincula.*

Left: *The White Tower.*

Grey's ghost is supposed to have appeared on Tower Green during the last execution carried out there, that of Robert Devereux, Earl of Essex, on 25 February 1601. Her ghost is also said to appear on the anniversary of her own execution, manifesting as a floating white figure drifting across Tower Green.

Another ghostly encounter recorded by Carkeet-James took place in 1864 and he states that it was vouched for by 'two senior officers in the King's Royal Rifle Corps'. A soldier from that regiment on sentry duty outside the Queen's House (then the Lieutenant's Lodgings) was found unconscious at his post and court-martialled. He claimed he had fainted in shock after challenging a white figure approaching his post through the early morning mist. Upon receiving no reply to his three challenges, he drove at the figure with his bayonet, which passed straight through the insubstantial shape. The sentry was acquitted when two witnesses corroborated his story. Another nineteenth-century tale says that a Yeoman Warder witnessed a bluish form drifting through the air in the direction of the Queen's House, and in 1933 a Guardsman near the Bloody Tower is supposed to have seen the apparition of a headless woman floating towards him.

The Chapel Royal of St Peter ad Vincula

The Chapel Royal of St Peter ad Vincula stands close to the scaffold site and is the final resting place for all who were executed there, as well as many of those killed on Tower Hill. Its grim name, which translates as St Peter in Chains, is perfectly apt for its setting but is coincidental for the dedication dates from long before the Tower was regularly used as a prison. A well-known story tells how many years ago, an Officer of the Guard saw lights burning within the locked chapel one night and climbed a ladder to peer in through one of the windows. The following account (from *Ghostly Visitors* by 'Spectre Stricken', 1882) describes what he saw:

> Slowly down the aisle moved a stately procession of knights and ladies, attired in ancient costumes; and in front walked an elegant female whose face was averted from him, but whose figure greatly resembled the one he had seen in reputed portraits of Anne Boleyn. After having repeatedly paced the chapel, the entire procession, together with the light, disappeared.

The White Tower

Tradition tells of an enormous, axe-shaped shadow that occasionally appears on Tower Green. Sometimes said to be associated with the terrible death of the Countess of Salisbury, the manifestation spreads across the grass until it stands defined against the walls of the White Tower, the ancient keep built by William the Conqueror (reigned 1066-1087) that is the core of the Tower of London. This formidable structure is positively steeped in supernatural lore.

At 11.45 p.m. one cold, moonless night in 1954, a sentry saw what looked like 'a puff of white smoke' emerge from the mouth of one of the old cannons that stood outside the White Tower. His account, published in the *Proceedings of the Society for Psychical Research* in 1960, describes how he watched as the smoke, 'hovered for a moment and made the shape of a square' before it, 'began to move along the railings of the path in [his] direction'. As it drew closer it changed shape again and the sentry, by now 'extremely frightened', left his post and hurried around the corner to summon a colleague on duty nearby. Together, they looked back and soon spotted the 'quivering and moving' shape, 'dangling on the wrong side of the steps leading up to the top of the wall'. Scared, the second sentry rushed back to his post to ring the alarm bell but by the time others arrived on the scene the apparition was no longer visible. Other guards patrolling outside the White Tower have reported hearing what sound like cries of pain coming from behind the doors to the basement, while inside various people have reported smelling the delicious (and appropriate) aroma of roasting beef, hearing the singing of a choir and even feeling the touch of a ghostly hand upon their shoulder. Access to the White Tower is via an external wooden staircase that leads up to what is referred to as the Ground Floor. Visitors ascending these steps pass an arch in the tower wall and peering into the dark space reveals a plaque relating to the two princes whose tale was told earlier with reference to the Bloody Tower. 'The tradition of the Tower,' reads this plaque, 'has always pointed out this as the stair under which the bones of Edward the 5th and his brother were found in Charles the 2nd's time and from whence they were removed to Westminster Abbey.'

Many of the White Tower's ghost stories were recorded by Graeme Rimer, Museum Assistant to the Armouries, in an article that appeared in *Strange Stories from the Tower of London*. According to Rimer, 'some years' before this article (which was penned around 1978) an experienced and conscientious DOE Custody Guard was patrolling what was at the time called the Record Room and is now the Line of Kings room. It was a hot summer night and the guard, nearing the end of his patrol, was getting ready to leave the White Tower but before he did so he sat down to remove his shoes for a moment. As he took off the first he heard a disembodied voice announce, 'There's only you and I here.' The guard leapt to his feet. 'You wait till I get this bloody shoe back on,' he replied, 'and there'll be only you here!'

Abbott (in his *Mysteries of the Tower of London*) records how at about 8.05 a.m. one day in 1978, an Armouries warden sweeping the floor in a room on the Ground Floor caught sight of a woman beyond one of the glass display cases. Puzzled because it was far too early for visitors, he walked around the case to get a better look and saw her move around the corner into the next room. He followed her but when he entered the room there was no sign of her. The only other way out was up the spiral staircase leading to the First Floor and so he started up the steps only to find the door at the top, leading into the Chapel of St John the Evangelist, locked and bolted. The warden summoned his colleagues and they searched the area but found no trace of the mysterious intruder.

Something similar happened to a guard in September 1980. At around 11.15 p.m. he was descending one of the spiral staircases when he glimpsed a woman above him walking up the steps. The central stone pillar obscured her upper half but he saw enough to know that she was wearing a black and grey skirt. It took a moment for the impact of what he had seen to register but when it did he turned around and hurried up after the figure. When he reached the top and the door leading to the round turret, he found it locked with no sign of the woman anywhere.

On the First Floor, strange events have been reported from the Norman chapel of St John the Evangelist. One custody guard told Joan Forman he had been cleaning the chapel on a hot day in 1985 when an icy draught suddenly blew past him as if, 'someone had opened a freezer door'. The chapel is also seemingly haunted by an overpowering smell of perfume although only a few people have been able to discern this. One was a very experienced custody guard who, according to Rimer, encountered the scent almost every night as he passed through the chapel on his regular patrol. Curiously, the smell was never noticeable until after midnight; it grew strongest during the early morning hours but faded completely by dawn. The guard described the smell as being like a cheap and stagnant perfume which he felt would make him physically sick if he was forced to breathe it in for very long. One suggestion is that the nauseating smell is the perfume of a phantom known as the White Lady who supposedly floats through rooms in the White Tower and has been seen standing at a window and waving.

But it was in the room adjoining the chapel that this guard experienced his most terrifying encounter with the unknown. This area is currently known as the Royal Castle but was at the time the Sword Room, and as usual his patrol took him into this room via the spiral staircase at the end farthest from the chapel. This night, however, the moment he set foot inside the room he felt an overwhelming physical pressure bearing down on and crushing him. Scarcely able to walk, the guard 'shuffled' towards the chapel but before he got that far he passed through an opening into the adjacent Sixteenth Century Gallery (now the Royal Armoury). As soon as he was out of the 'Sword Room' the pressure lifted. Around three years later, he experienced exactly the same horrifying sensation, as if some mysterious presence once again objected to his being there.

Visitors to the White Tower make their exit via the lowest level, now known as the Basement, and a final ghostly tale from the White Tower is unusual in that it points not towards the past but the future. At 2.30 p.m. on 17 July 1974, a terrorist bomb ripped through the Mortar Room (now the Artillery Room), while it was packed with tourists, including many children. One woman was killed in the blast and numerous visitors received horrific injuries. While researching her book on time and timeslips (*The Mask of Time*), Joan Forman was told a strange story by two women who had visited the White Tower several weeks before the explosion. As she was leaving the tower on 20 April 1974, 'T' remarked to her friend 'R' that she could hear children shouting and crying somewhere nearby. 'R' could not hear this and 'T' became irritated at her friend's inexplicable failure to hear the perfectly clear sounds. The affair was forgotten until news of the bombing was reported a few weeks later, and 'T' could not help but wonder if the cries she had heard had been some form of precognition of the distress of children caught up in the terror and confusion of that July afternoon.

The Waterloo Barracks

As you exit the White Tower you find yourself facing the Waterloo Barracks, built while the Duke of Wellington was Constable of the Tower (1826-1852). Originally used as accommodation for almost 1,000 soldiers, this block now houses the Crown Jewels, including the cursed Koh-i-Noor diamond, set in the Crown of Queen Elizabeth the Queen Mother. It is no coincidence that this is a crown intended for a woman for according to legend a man possessing this diamond is doomed to misfortune and violent death.

At around 4.15 a.m. on 24 April 1980, two sentries on patrol outside the Waterloo Barracks spotted a tall dark figure at the east end of the building and gave chase. The figure vanished near the steps leading to the Casemates (the collective name for the private homes built between the Tower's inner and outer walls). Also at the building's east end, on 30 July the same year a Yeoman Warder left his second floor flat in the middle of the day, stepped into the corridor and clearly heard a voice remark, 'Oh, sorry!' Turning, he saw a man dressed in a suit and wearing a brown trilby hat of the sort popular in the 1940s. The man was standing no more than a few feet away by some swing doors, one of which had been propped open, and a moment later he turned and walked through the opening. Wondering where the stranger could be heading, the Yeoman Warder walked after him but found no sign of him anywhere.

Possibly the same mysterious figure was spotted inside the Waterloo Barracks at about 3 a.m. one cold morning that September. A sentry patrolling the front of the building had the uncomfortable feeling of being watched but, seeing nobody, he continued his patrol. At the far end of the long building he turned and began to make his way back, still sensing that something was amiss, and then through the glass windows of the doorway he spotted a man crouching and looking at him. The figure, clearly silhouetted against the brightly burning hallway lights, reacted quickly, moving away as if realising that it had been seen. Knowing that all the doors, internal and external, were securely locked the sentry radioed for assistance and the entire building was thoroughly searched but, of course, the intruder was never found.

Some suggest the Waterloo Barracks ghost is that of a German spy executed in the Tower during the Second World War. Josef Jakobs parachuted into England on the night of 31 January 1941 but broke an ankle on landing and was swiftly captured. On 4 August he was found guilty of being a spy and sentenced to death. Taken to the Tower of London he was held prisoner in a room at the east end of the Waterloo Barracks, on the same floor and close to where the man in a trilby hat was seen. Early in the morning of 14 August 1941, Jakobs was escorted to the miniature rifle range that once stood in the Casemates between the Martin and Constable towers, where he was shot through the heart by a firing squad. Interestingly, the steps down which the tall dark figure vanished, lead to this same vicinity.

The Martin Tower

For two centuries, the Martin Tower housed the Crown Jewels and so was known as the Jewel Tower. This tower to the east of the Waterloo Barracks is the location of the Tower of London's two most celebrated supernatural tales, both recorded by no less credible a person than Edward Lenthal Swifte, the Keeper of the Crown Jewels. He experienced the first incident personally, recounting it years later in *Notes & Queries* (1860):

One Saturday night in October, 1817, about the 'witching hour', I was at supper with my wife, her sisters, and our little boy, in the sitting-room of the Jewel House, which – then comparatively modernised – is said to have been the 'doleful prison' of Anne Boleyn, and of the ten bishops whom Oliver Cromwell piously accommodated therein. […] The room was – as it still is – irregularly shaped, having three doors and two windows, which last are cut nearly nine feet deep into the outer wall; between these is a chimney-piece, projecting far into the room, and (then) surmounted with a large oil-painting. On the night in question the doors were all closed, heavy and dark cloth curtains were let down over the windows, and the only light in the room was that of two candles on the table; I sat at the foot of the table, my son on my right hand, his mother fronting the chimney-piece, and her sister on the opposite side. I had offered a glass of wine and water to my wife, when, on putting it to her lips, she paused, and exclaimed, 'Good God! what is that?' I looked up, and saw a cylindrical figure, like a glass-tube, seemingly about the thickness of my arm, and hovering between the ceiling and the table; its contents appeared to be a dense fluid, white and pale azure, like to the gathering of a summer-cloud, and incessantly mingling within the cylinder. This lasted about two minutes, when it began slowly to move *before* my sister-in-law; then, following the oblong-shape of the table, *before* my son and myself; passing *behind* my wife, it paused for a moment over her right shoulder (observe, there was no mirror opposite to her in which she could there behold it). Instantly she crouched down, and with both hands covering her shoulder, she shrieked out, 'O Christ! it has seized me!' Even now, while writing, I feel the fresh horror of that moment. I caught up my chair, struck at the wainscot behind her, rushed up-stairs to the other children's room, and told the terrified nurse what I had seen. Meanwhile the other domestics had hurried into the parlour, where their mistress recounted to them the scene, even as I was detailing it above stairs.

The marvel of all this is enhanced by the fact that *neither my sister-in-law nor my son beheld this 'appearance'*.

Lenthal Swifte's description generated much correspondence and in one of his replies he reported the sinister story of the phantom bear that caused the death of a sentry. According to various accounts, this episode occurred only a few days after the above incident, or in either 1815 or 1816:

Above: *The Waterloo Barracks.*

Right: *The Martin Tower.*

Left: *Northumberland's Walk, looking north towards the Martin Tower.*

Below: *The Constable Tower.*

One of the night sentries at the Jewel Office, a man who was in perfect health and spirits, and was singing and whistling up to the moment of the occurrence, was alarmed by a figure like a huge bear issuing from under the Jewel Room door. He thrust at it with his bayonet, which stuck in the door […]; he dropped in a fit, and was carried senseless to the guard-room.

When on the morrow I saw the unfortunate soldier in the main guard-room, his fellow-sentinel was also there, and testified to having seen him at his post just before the alarm, awake and alert, and had even spoken to him. I saw the unfortunate man again on the following day, but changed beyond my recognition; in another day or two, the brave and steady soldier, who would have mounted a breach, or led a forlorn hope with unshaken nerves, *died* – at the presence of a shadow.

Support for this tale came from a Mr George Offor, who had also been stationed at the Tower at this time and who wrote:

Before the burning of the armouries there was a paved yard in front of the Jewel House, from which a gloomy and ghost-like doorway led down a flight of steps to the Mint. Some strange noises were heard in this gloomy corner; and on a dark night at twelve the sentry saw a figure like a bear cross the pavement and disappear down the steps. This so terrified him that he fell, and in a few hours after, having recovered sufficiently to tell the tale, he died.

Was this strange figure really a phantom bear? If so, perhaps it is a reminder of the days when the Tower of London housed the Royal Menagerie. This was already in existence by the thirteenth century and the royal collection of wild animals was kept here for hundreds of years until the last beasts were removed to the Zoological Gardens in Regent's Park in 1834.

Northumberland's Walk and the Constable Tower
In 1605 Henry Percy, the ninth Earl of Northumberland, was arrested for complicity in the Gunpowder Plot and the following year he was tried and sentenced to life imprisonment in the Tower of London, although he was eventually released in 1621. Held in the Martin Tower he was allowed to take his exercise upon the walls to either side, which are now known as Northumberland's Walk. Although he did not die here, his ghost supposedly remains and several sentries have reported seeing it still pacing these ramparts.

South of the Martin Tower and connected to it by Northumberland's Walk, stands the Constable Tower. Here, since 1973, a strong smell of sweat, leather and horse – the smell of a rider returned from a hard gallop – has from time to time been reported.

The Salt Tower
The Salt Tower stands at the south-east corner of the Inner Ward. During the reign of Elizabeth I the first-floor chamber here saw much use as a prison cell for Catholic priests, and the walls still bear inscriptions scratched into them by these victims of religious persecution. One inscription bears the name of the English Jesuit Henry Walpole and the names of the saints to whom he prayed for courage. During his imprisonment at the Tower Walpole was frequently subjected to torture on the rack, but despite his tremendous agonies he refused to give up the names of his Catholic contacts and in 1595 was sent to York for execution. Some suspect it was his spirit that frightened a Yeoman Warder here late one afternoon in 1973. The Yeoman Warder had recently been reading a book condemning the Jesuits and now he stood in the same gloomy chamber where members of that order had been incarcerated, contemplating the carved inscriptions. Inexplicably, a strange glow illuminated the room and a moment later he felt something touch

The Salt Tower.

the back of his neck. Overcome with fear he fled the ancient chamber, racing down the stone steps and out into the welcoming open air.

And it was just outside the Salt Tower that a young Welsh Guardsman named Johns was on duty in 1957 when his attention was attracted by a rattling noise from somewhere above him. It was around 3 a.m. on the cold, damp morning of 12 February, the 403rd anniversary of the execution of Lady Jane Grey, and Johns looked up to see a 'white shapeless form' on the tower's battlemented roof some 40ft above him. As he watched, the shape formed itself into the likeness of a young woman. Shocked, he summoned a colleague who also witnessed the apparition. 'I thought I was seeing things,' Johns stated afterwards. 'The ghost stood between the battlements. I went to tell the other guard and as I pointed to the battlements the figure appeared again.'

So many strange stories come from the Tower of London that after a while they begin to seem almost normal. A Welsh Guards officer who later commented on the above incident gave a simple statement, 'Guardsman Johns is convinced he saw a ghost. Speaking for the regiment, our attitude is, "All right, so you say you saw a ghost. Let's leave it at that."'

CHAPTER SEVEN

THE EAST: GHOSTS OF JACK THE RIPPER'S VICTIMS

Mary Ann Nichols

There is a theory that powerful emotions can somehow imprint themselves onto a place and that at least some ghost sightings can be explained by people 'tuning in' to these recordings of past events. If there is any truth in this at all, perhaps it is not surprising that the violent murders and mutilations that brought horror to London's East End in 1888's 'Autumn of Terror' left behind them many strange stories.

The night of Thursday 30 August 1888 was especially miserable. Thunder had rumbled over east London earlier that afternoon and since then squalls of rain had been lashing the squalid Whitechapel streets, falling from a sky stained red by fires blazing at the docks. Located just to the east of the City, this part of London lay in terrible contrast to that prosperous square mile. Dirty, poverty-stricken and overcrowded, much of the district was a stinking warren of dark alleyways, tiny courtyards and narrow cobbled streets, and it was through this that Mary Ann 'Polly' Nichols was walking, probably looking for 'trade'. Aged forty-three, a little over 5ft tall with greying brown hair and missing several teeth, Polly had sunk into alcoholism and prostitution since the breakdown of her marriage several years before. At around half past midnight on the Friday morning, she stumbled out of the Frying Pan public house on the corner of Brick Lane and Thrawl Street. She had intended to sleep at the lodging house at No.18 Thrawl Street where she shared a room with three other women but at around 1.20 a.m. the deputy in charge there turned her away because she could not pay for her bed for the night. 'Never mind,' she replied drunkenly, indicating her new black straw bonnet. 'I'll soon get me doss money. See what a jolly bonnet I've got now.' With that, she staggered back out into the darkness, looking for a client to earn herself the few pennies she needed.

The last recorded sighting of her alive was at about 2.30 a.m. as she stumbled off east down Whitechapel Road. Her mutilated body was discovered at approximately 3.40 a.m. by a carman named Charles Cross as he headed to work down a narrow and dimly lit stretch of Buck's Row (since re-named Durward Street, just to the north of Whitechapel Underground station). She was lying on her back on the ground, outside the gates to a stable yard, with her skirts pulled up over her knees. In the gloom, Cross and a second man, Robert Paul, did not notice that Polly's throat had been violently slashed twice from left to right and her abdomen torn open, exposing her intestines. She had become the first definite victim of the killer that history remembers as Jack the Ripper.

Durward Street (formerly Bucks Row) today. Mary Ann Nichols's body was discovered on the ground where the cars are parked to the left in this picture. The large building behind this spot was a school in 1888.

Several years after Polly's murder, Elliott O'Donnell visited Whitechapel in 1895 and several local residents told him that, 'appalling screams and groans uttered by no living human being were sometimes heard at night' in the streets where the Ripper had slaughtered his victims. In Bucks Row itself, he was informed, 'a huddled-up figure, like that of a woman, emitting from all over it a ghostly light, was frequently to be seen lying in the gutter'. Peter Underwood, in his *Jack the Ripper: One Hundred Years of Mystery* adds that there were tales of animals reacting oddly to that part of Buck's Row. Horses would flare their nostrils, flatten their ears and pull up sharply, and for years afterwards dogs would strain at their leashes to avoid the spot where Polly Nichols's body was discovered.

Annie Chapman

Just over one week after Polly's death there was a second horrible murder. The victim was another prostitute, forty-seven-year-old Annie Chapman, known to many as 'Dark Annie'. Like Polly, she did not have enough money to pay for her night's lodging and so in the early hours of Saturday 8 September 1888 she was walking the Whitechapel streets in search of a paying customer. A witness later claimed she saw Annie talking to a man outside No. 29 Hanbury Street at around 5.30 a.m. that day and described him as aged over forty, looking 'like a foreigner' and

Hanbury Street today.

being of 'shabby genteel' appearance, wearing a deerstalker hat and possibly a dark overcoat. At around the same time, a young man living next door at No. 27 Hanbury Street walked into his backyard and overheard people talking on the other side of the tall wooden fence. He heard a woman say, 'No' but thought little of it, even when something fell heavily against the fence a few minutes later. At around 6 a.m. that morning, John Davis, one of the many tenants of No. 29, walked into that house's backyard and discovered Annie's body. Her head had been almost severed by two deep cuts, her abdomen ripped open and her intestines pulled out and draped across her shoulder. Her uterus had been removed altogether and was missing. Dr George Bagster Phillips, who performed the post-mortem, declared that the injuries would probably have taken at least fifteen minutes to inflict. He also said that in his opinion the killer possessed some anatomical knowledge, a suggestion that remains the subject of much controversy.

Shortly after Annie's murder, stories began to circulate telling of the apparitions of a man and a woman seen in the vicinity of No. 29 Hanbury Street. These reports continued until at least the 1930s and in around 1960 Peter Underwood spoke to someone who claimed to remember seeing these apparitions on four occasions, usually around the autumn. By coincidence, the gentleman's name was Mr Chapman, and he lived in Hanbury Street immediately opposite No. 29. One morning, having risen early to get ready for working an early shift, he looked out of his bedroom window and spotted a couple disappearing into the doorway of No. 29. He caught only a fleeting glimpse but was certain that the woman had worn an old-fashioned long skirt and the man a heavy greatcoat and tall, wide-brimmed hat. He saw them again another morning as he was leaving his front door. The couple were walking on the other side of the street and they entered No. 29 just as he set off to work through the rain. It took a few moments before he realised that he had heard absolutely no sound of footsteps from the couple as they passed by. A few months later he saw them for the third time. As he looked out of his bedroom window early one morning he spotted the two figures walking along the street and he immediately called for his wife to come and look. She hurried over, reaching the window just as Mr Chapman saw the couple disappear into No. 29's doorway. His wife was a moment too late to catch sight of the figures themselves but she told her husband that she should surely have been able to see the door close behind them yet both the left-hand door leading through to the backyard and the right-hand door leading to the house had been closed when she looked. With a start, Mr Chapman realised that he also had seen neither door open or close; the figures had simply disappeared into the doorway. He saw them for the final time several years later. On this occasion he was accompanied by his brother who was working the same early morning shift that day and as they started to walk along Hanbury Street towards Wilkes Street Mr Chapman saw the couple on the other side of the road. He nudged his brother, indicating their presence to him with a jerk of the head. The couple were just coming up to No. 29 and the moment they passed by, Mr Chapman turned around to get a better look. There was no sign of the couple anywhere and when he asked his brother what he had thought of the man and woman he received a puzzled reply, 'Saw who? I didn't see anyone … I thought I heard the sound of footsteps on the other side of the road and I thought that was what you were trying to tell me …'

Underwood also spoke to a man named Thomas, another Hanbury Street resident, who told him of something that happened to him in around 1930. As Thomas walked past No. 29 one night, the door leading through to the backyard was open and through it he heard panting and muffled voices, mixed with what sounded like a struggle. Fearing someone was in trouble, he nervously entered and crept down the short passage until he stood at the back of the house at the top of the steps leading down into the yard, and peered around the back door. The darkened backyard was deserted yet he could still hear the sounds, more clearly now that he was closer to their source. Someone was breathing heavily and someone else was gasping for breath. There was a pause – then the sound of something being dragged, then silence. Thomas was by now terrified, for as he listened he had been moving through the yard looking everywhere, even over the fence, and there was absolutely nothing to be seen. Worse still, it was now obvious that the sounds had emanated from a very specific place: the exact spot where Annie Chapman's body had been discovered.

Today, the site of No. 29 on the north side of Hanbury Street is covered by buildings that formerly belonged to the Truman Brewery and there are stories that Annie's phantom was occasionally spotted standing by the walls of a storeroom, once again on the spot where her body was found. It is also said that anyone in the brewery's boardroom at 6 a.m. on the anniversary of her murder might have felt a chill draught blow through the air. Another chill breeze was reported inside a nearby pub in the mid-1970s. The Ten Bells stands in Commercial Street on the corner of Fournier Street and is only a short distance from Hanbury Street. When the landlord realised how close his pub stood to the murder site, he changed its name to the Jack the Ripper to draw in passing tourists, and decorated the interior walls with such items as *Police Gazette* articles on the crimes. Later, he said, he was surprised to learn that the victim's surname had been Chapman for this was his own wife's maiden name. He also claimed that Annie Chapman's spirit haunted his pub, and that she was responsible for several strange incidents including switching the radio on and off and the ghostly breeze previously mentioned. The pub's name has since reverted to the Ten Bells, the name by which it was known in 1888.

The Ten Bells public house would have been a familiar sight to the Ripper's victims.

Elizabeth Stride

Elizabeth Stride's married surname may have been the origin of her nickname: 'Long Liz'. Born Elisabeth Gustafsdotter in 1843 on a farm in Torslanda near Gothenburg in Sweden, she moved to London in 1866. Those who knew her described her as a very quiet woman, helpful, neat and clean, although she was also charged several times with being drunk and disorderly. She claimed she had been caught up in the *Princess Alice* disaster of 1878 when that passenger steamer collided with the collier *Bywell Castle* on the Thames near Woolwich with the loss of between 600 and 700 lives. According to Liz, she was injured in the accident and her husband and children were among those killed but it is thought that she invented this story to conceal a broken marriage or to garner sympathy. By 1885 she was living with a waterside labourer named Michael Kidney in a stormy on-off relationship, earning a meagre income through sewing and charring and occasionally supplementing this by working in the evening as a prostitute. For the final few days of her life she had been staying at a lodging house at No. 32 Flower and Dean Street, probably after another quarrel with Kidney. At about 11 p.m. on Saturday 29 September 1888, she was seen leaving the Bricklayer's Arms public house on Settle Street in the company of a young man, and several people later reported spotting her that night with someone who may or may not have been the same person. Around 1 a.m. on the Sunday a jewellery salesman named Louis Diemschütz drove his pony and cart through a set of large wooden gates into Dutfield's Yard – little more than a dark space containing a sack warehouse and a disused stables on the west side of the narrow Berner Street (now named Henriques Street, leading south from Commercial Road). Suddenly, the pony shied to the left and Diemschütz looked down to see what the obstruction was. The yard was pitch black but by probing with his whip and striking a match he could just about make out a body lying on the ground.

Around one month later, according to an account recorded in *Elliott O'Donnell's Casebook of Ghosts*, a Whitechapel tradesman walking north along Berner Street late one night heard moaning and groaning from somewhere close by but could not make out where the harrowing sounds were coming from. He ran for help and a small crowd quickly gathered, attracted by the commotion. Still unable to decide precisely where the sounds had come from the tradesman was about to knock on the door to a house when a woman in the crowd called out to him, 'It's no good knocking there, guv'nor. Them sounds don't come from that house, they're in the street 'ere – we've often 'eered 'em since poor Lizzie was done to death close to this 'ere spot'.

Liz Stride's throat had been cut from left to right, severing her windpipe, but unlike the previous victims there were no other signs of mutilation and the body was still warm, with blood flowing from her wound. Diemschütz's unexpected arrival may have interrupted the Ripper before he had finished and the killer's frustration at failing to complete his work could explain why he claimed his fourth victim that very same night.

Catherine Eddowes

Catherine 'Kate' Eddowes was in her forties and bore the initials 'TC' on her left forearm, tattooed there in blue ink in reference to her former lover Thomas Conway. By 1881, Kate and Thomas had separated and she was living with an Irish porter named John Kelly in Cooney's lodging house at No. 55 Flower and Dean Street. Despite their poverty, the couple were reasonably happy together. She scraped a living by charring and hawking, and probably also solicited from time to time to bring in a little extra money. Kate and Kelly spent much of the

Right: *Henriques Street (formerly Berner Street) today. Dutfield's Yard where Elizabeth Stride's body was discovered was located on the right-hand side of the road, at around the centre of this photo.*

Below: *Mitre Square today. Catherine Eddowes's body lay close to where the benches are sited to the right in this picture.*

September of 1888 picking hops in Kent, but earned little and by the morning of Saturday 29 September they were back in London and broke. They pawned a pair of Kelly's boots for 2s 6d and used the money to buy food, eating it together in the lodging house kitchen. That afternoon Kate told Kelly she was going to Bermondsey to visit Annie, her daughter by Thomas, to borrow some cash. The plan could not have succeeded for Annie had moved since her last visit, but Kate must have acquired money from somewhere because by 8 p.m. she was roaring drunk and attracting a crowd in Aldgate High Street with her impersonation of a fire engine. Arrested for being drunk and disorderly she was taken to Bishopsgate police station and locked in a cell. She slept for a time but by 12.15 a.m. she was awake again and could be heard singing quietly to herself. At around 1 a.m. on Sunday 30 September, PC George Hutt decided that Kate was sober enough to be released and escorted her out of the station, asking her to close the door after her. 'All right,' she replied, 'Good night, old cock.' These were her last recorded words.

When PC Watkins, walking his beat, arrived in Mitre Square at around 1.45 a.m., he spotted something that had not been there on his last visit just fifteen minutes earlier. Lying on the cobbled ground in the dark shadows of the square's southern corner was Kate's still-warm body, resting on her back in a pool of blood. Her throat had been slashed from left to right, her face horrifically mutilated and her stomach ripped open. Most of her intestines had been drawn out and placed over her right shoulder, although a section about 2ft long had been cut away and deliberately positioned between her body and left arm. The post mortem later revealed that her left kidney and part of her uterus had been cut out and were missing.

Mitre Square still exists and retains its name although its character has changed much since 1888 when the walls of the buildings that surrounded it then loomed much closer and gave the square a claustrophobic atmosphere. According to the stories told, many walking through this small square, usually in late September and often on the actual anniversary of the murder, have spied something on the ground in the shadows of what became known as Ripper's Corner. Sometimes they initially think that they are looking at a bundle of clothes but when they get closer they realise it is a body, the gruesome apparition of Kate's corpse lying on the ground on the spot where she was killed. (Mitre Square actually lies within the City of London rather than the East End but this tale is included here for the sake of clarity.)

Mary Jane Kelly

Mary Jane – or 'Marie Jeanette' – Kelly was around twenty-five years old. Originally from Limerick in Ireland, she was pretty and retained her fresh-faced looks despite a hard life. Already a widow following her collier husband's death in a pit explosion, Mary came to London in 1884 and may have worked for a time in a high-class brothel in the West End. One of her 'gentlemen' had taken her to live in Paris, she said, but she had not enjoyed it and so had returned to London a fortnight later. By November 1888, she had been living for several months at No. 13 Miller's Court (actually a single room at the back of No. 26 Dorset Street), which she shared with an Irish cockney named Joseph Barnett. Barnett hated the idea of Mary working as a prostitute and would give her money when he could rather than let her walk the streets, but after a fierce row on 30 October – sparked by Mary allowing another prostitute to sleep in their room – she and Barnett separated. Afterwards they remained on reasonably friendly terms but Barnett had lost his job at Billingsgate Fish Market a few months earlier and had little money to share with her, and on the evening of Thursday 8 November Mary was behind with her rent. Although she was terrified of the Ripper her need to earn money drove her out that night to look for clients.

Looking east along the alley where Dorset Street once stood.

The following day, Friday 9 November, was the day of the Lord Mayor's Show. That morning, Mary's landlord, John McCarthy, sent his assistant, Thomas Bowyer, to No. 13 Miller's Court to collect the 29s Mary owed. Bowyer knocked twice on the door but received no reply and so he walked around to the side to peer in through the window. What he saw inside was so terrible that he immediately raced back to fetch McCarthy, who afterwards stated that the scene, 'looked more like the work of a devil than of a man'. Perhaps because this was the only Ripper murder committed indoors, giving the killer time to carry out his work undisturbed, it was the most shocking of them all. Mary Kelly had quite literally been butchered. What was left of her lay on her back on a bed soaked in blood. Her throat had been slashed right down to her spinal column and her face mutilated, with her cheeks, eyebrows, ears and nose partially removed. Her breasts had been cut off, her body opened and her viscera cut out. Various body parts had been placed under her head and around her body and the bedside table was piled with flesh.

Curiously, one of Mary's neighbours later testified that she saw and even spoke to Mary several hours after she must have been killed. Some time between 8.00 and 8.30 a.m. on 9 November, Mrs Caroline Maxwell, who lived at No. 14 Dorset Street, spotted Mary standing by the entrance to Miller's Court and called out to her. She asked Mary why she was up and about so early, to which Mary replied that she was ill and that she had just drunk a glass of beer and vomited it up. Mrs Maxwell asserted that she saw Mary again at around a quarter to nine that morning, talking to a man outside the Britannia pub, but her claims were put down to a case of mistaken identity.

Dorset Street no longer exists and where it stood is now a nondescript alley running alongside a multi-storey car park on Commercial Street, but while it remained people claimed the site was haunted by Mary Kelly's ghost. She was said to manifest as a woman dressed in black clothing who was occasionally spotted walking through the door of her old home or gazing out from the window as eerie sounds came from within. In 1959, a lady claimed in a television interview that her mother moved into No.13 Miller's Court shortly after the murder. 'There was a picture of the Crucifixion on the wall,' she said, 'and behind it was a bloody imprint of a hand. No matter how many times it was painted over it always showed through.' It seems a fitting tale, for despite the many changes this part of London has undergone since those few terrifying weeks in 1888, the bloody imprint of the Ripper's horrific crimes has never been completely erased.

While Mary Kelly is widely held to have been his final victim, Jack the Ripper was never caught – at least not that has been officially acknowledged – and his identity has never been definitively established. Despite countless theories his ultimate fate remains unknown, but according to one legend he committed suicide by throwing himself into the River Thames from Westminster Bridge (see 'Westminster Bridge', p. 59). As has already been mentioned, his own ghost is sometimes said to appear there on New Year's Eve, dressed in the now familiar yet unlikely attire of top hat and frock coat, and thus the Ripper himself joins his victims as yet another phantom in the long list of ghostly tales from London.

APPENDIX

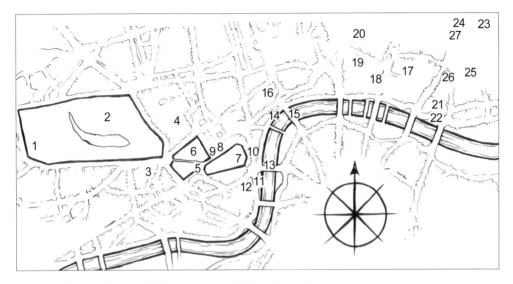

Map of London. (Anthony Wallis www.ant-wallis-illustration.co.uk)

KEY TO MAP:

THE WEST: FROM KENSINGTON TO
    MAYFAIR
1. Kensington Palace
2. Hyde Park
3. The Grenadier
4. No. 50 Berkeley Square

ROYAL LONDON: AROUND THE
    GREEN PARK & ST JAMES'S PARK
5. Buckingham Palace
6. The Green Park
7. St James's Park
8. St James's Palace
9. Clarence House

WESTMINSTER: POLITICIANS &
    PRIESTS
10. No. 10 Downing Street
11. The Houses of Parliament
12. Westminster Abbey
13. Westminster Bridge

THE RIVER THAMES: AROUND THE
    VICTORIA EMBANKMENT
14. Cleopatra's Needle
15. Waterloo Bridge
16. The Theatre Royal, Drury Lane

THE CITY: LONDON'S HEART
17. The Bank of England
18. St Paul's Cathedral
19. The Old Bailey
20. Smithfield Market

THE TOWER: TOWER HILL & THE
    TOWER OF LONDON
21. Tower Hill
22. The Tower of London

THE EAST: GHOSTS OF JACK THE
    RIPPER'S VICTIMS
23. Mary Ann Nichols
24. Annie Chapman
25. Elizabeth Stride
26. Catherine Eddowes
27. Mary Jane Kelly

BIBLIOGRAPHY

Abbott, G., *Ghosts of the Tower of London,* Heinemann, London, 1980

Abbott, G., *Mysteries of the Tower of London*, Hendon Publishing, Lancashire, 1998

Ackroyd, Peter, *London: The Biography*, Vintage, London, 2001

Anderson, Sir Robert, K.C.B, *The Lighter Side of My Official Life*, Hodder & Stoughton, London, 1910

Bardens, Dennis, *Ghosts & Hauntings*, Senate, London, 1997 (originally published 1965)

Braddock, Joseph, *Haunted Houses*, Cedric Chivers Ltd, Bath, 1966 edn

Brooks, J.A., *Ghosts of London*, Jarrold Publishing, Norwich, 1991 (second edn)

Carkeet-James, Colonel E.H., OBE, MC, *His Majesty's Tower of London*, Staple Press Ltd, London, 1950

Chambers, Robert (ed), *The Book of Days*, W. & R. Chambers, 1869

Forman, Joan, *Haunted Royal Homes*, Jarrold Publishing, Norwich, 1992

Green, Andrew, *Our Haunted Kingdom*, Wolfe Publishing Ltd, London, 1973

Green, Celia, *Analysis of Spontaneous Cases*, Appendix B, Proceedings of the Society for Psychical Research, Volume 53, Nov 1960

Hallam, Jack, *Ghosts of London*, Wolfe Publishing Ltd, London, 1975

Harper, Charles G., *Haunted Houses*, Senate, London, 1994 (originally published 1907)

Hopkins, R. Thurston, *Ghosts Over England*, Meridian, London, 1953

Jones, Richard, *Haunted London*, New Holland, London, 2004

Jones, Steve, *London … The Sinister Side*, Tragical History Tours (Publications) Ltd, Kent, 1986

Ludham, Harry (ed), *Elliott O'Donnell's Casebook of Ghosts*, W. Foulsham & Co., Ltd, London, 1969

Macqueen-Pope, W., *Pillars of Drury Lane,* Hutchinson, London, 1955

Macqueen-Pope, W., *Theatre Royal, Drury Lane*, W.H. Allen, London, 1945

Middleton, Jessie Adelaide, *The Grey Ghost Book*, Eveleigh Nash, London, 1912

O'Donnell, Elliott, *Ghosts of London*, E.P. Dutton & Co. Inc, New York, 1933

O'Donnell, Elliott, *Great Thames Mysteries,* Selwyn & Blount, London, 1930

O'Donnell, Elliott, *Haunted Britain*, Consul, London, 1963

O'Donnell, Elliot, *More Haunted Houses of London*, Eveleigh Nash, London, 1920

Owen, George and Sims, Victor, *Science and the Spook*, Dennis Dobson, London, 1971

Playfair, Guy Lyon, *The Haunted Pub Guide*, Javelin Books, Poole, Dorset, 1987

Rimer, Graeme, 'A Ghost Guide to the Armouries', *Strange Stories from the Tower of London*, 'British History Illustrated' supplement, Historical Times Ltd, *c.* 1978

'Spectre Stricken'*, Ghostly Visitors: a series of authentic narratives*, E.W. Allen, London, 1882

Spencer, John and Anne, *The Encyclopedia of Ghosts and Spirits*, Headline, London, 1992

Underwood, Peter, *Haunted London*, Fontana, London, 1973

Underwood, Peter, *Jack the Ripper: One Hundred Years of Mystery*, Javelin Books, London, 1988

Underwood, Peter, *The Ghost Hunter's Guide*, Javelin Books, London, 1988

Walker, Charles, *Strange Britain*, Brian Todd Publishing House Ltd, 1989

Wardroper, John, *Wicked Ernest*, Shelfmark Books, London, 2002

Westwood, Jennifer, *Albion: A Guide to Legendary Britain*, Paladin, London, 1987

Other local titles published by Tempus

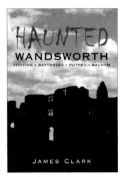

Haunted Wandsworth

JAMES CLARK

This collection of stories contains both well-known and hitherto unpublished tales of the ghosts, mysteries and legends of Wandsworth. From the spectral son of Marie Antoinette to a haunting at the Battersea Dogs and Cats home, this scary selection of ghostly goings-on is bound to captivate anyone interested in the supernatural history of the area.

978 07524 4070 5

Haunted Kent

JANET CAMERON

Haunted Kent contains spooky stories from around the county, including the hunchbacked monk at Boughton Malherbe, the black dog of Leeds and the well-known tale of Lady Blanche of Rochester Castle. This fascinating collection of strange sightings and happenings in the county's streets, churches, public houses and country lanes is sure to appeal to anyone wanting to know why Kent is known as the most haunted county in England.

988 07524 3605 0

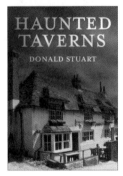

Haunted Taverns

DONALD STUART

Take an A-Z tour of haunted taverns around Britain. From hair-raising tales about a fourteenth-century pub with its own ghost duck, the phantom who leaves a strong smell of rum and tobacco throughout an ancient inn, the beer jug that fills itself up in the middle of the night to a Devil's dog the size of a calf that disappears into the walls of the old inn it haunts, this book will bring goose-bumps to those who dare open its cover.

978 07524 4347 8

Haunted Guildford

PHILIP HUTCHINSON

Heart-stopping accounts of apparitions abound in this anthology of old and new ghost stories from around Guildford. From tales of a piano-playing spirit at Guildford Museum and a spectral monk who wanders up Friary Street, to stories of a poltergeist at the Three Pigeons public house and sightings of a ghostly woman on Whitmoor Common, this selection is sure to appeal to anyone interested in the darker history of Guildford.

097 07524 3826 9

If you are interested in purchasing other books published by Tempus, or in case you have difficulty finding any Tempus books in your local bookshop, you can also place orders directly through our website

www.tempus-publishing.com